THE WAR INSIDE

FINDING VICTORY OVER ALCOHOL

JORDAN NORTHRUP

Good Bless you Joe!

Reddington
Press

To all who are
fighting a war inside,
there is hope.

May this book point you to Jesus, our Hope.

ACKNOWLEDGMENTS

Writing this book was no easy thing. Pulling back the curtain on my personal struggles and pain meant dredging up old wounds in the writing process. This book required a tough look in the mirror and a lot of honesty, but the reflection was worth it in the hope that this story will minister to others.

Many people impacted my story along the way, for better or worse, and I've changed their names in this book out of consideration to them. However, two people played an especially important role in my story as it continues today, and they influenced the creation of this book in the best of ways. I would like to offer a special by-name thank you to them.

Donn, thank you for being my counselor, mentor, and friend for all these years. I was a broken mess when we first met, but your wisdom and counsel pointed me back to the Lord and kept me focused on getting right with Him. You believed in me even when I didn't believe in myself. You helped me realize a new identify in Christ that was not bound to my mistakes. Thank you for walking side by side with me along this long and hard, but wonderful and redemptive journey.

Nadia, you are truly my soul mate and best friend. We had

not met when I was living out this story, but you embraced my past and never doubted the work God had done to change my life. Words cannot fully express how much you mean to me. Thank you for being my editor and encouraging this endeavor. This book is as much yours as it is mine.

PROLOGUE

I survived three deployments to war and multiple brushes with death, yet it was the war with alcohol raging inside that nearly claimed my life. By the time I was 34 years old, I had been abusing alcohol for fourteen years. It began when I was an undergraduate at college. What started as social drinking to fit in on campus soon progressed to full blown alcohol abuse.

On any given weekend, I consumed more alcohol than most people drink in a month, or even two. Later, as an officer in the Marine Corps, I still could not conquer alcohol's hold on my life. Duty and honor-bound, I fulfilled missions and gave my all to the Marine Corps, but in my personal life, short-sightedness still claimed my attention and I focused on little else beyond extended weekends of partying and getting wasted.

Although I was never diagnosed as an alcoholic in the clinical definition of the term, I was certainly addicted. Poor life choices and a willful disregard for the Lord caused me to turn to alcohol to cope with life's problems.

I ended up feeling lost, broken, and terrified about my future. I imagined life in ten years and could see myself on the streets with no place to live, no job, no family or friends, and worst of all, no hope. I was afraid that people would discover my secret and disown me. I was afraid that I would lose my position in the Marine Corps and my job once my superiors and co-workers discovered my habit. I was afraid that the people of the church I attended would find out and tell me that I was no longer welcome to worship with them.

Above all, I was afraid that I would become worthless, sinking so low that even my humanity would be in question. Yet even with these dark worries, the next weekend and the next binge were all I could think about. I didn't like reality and my only escape was a drunken stupor where I didn't have to deal with my problems or face the person I saw in the mirror.

After fourteen years of alcohol abuse, I felt like a dead man walking. I couldn't go on any longer; I was physically, emotionally, and spiritually worn out. I had reached the end of my rope with no place to go. I felt trapped. Enslaved to the bottle just as if I was weighed down by chains, and I couldn't shake off the invisible chains no matter how hard I tried. Death, either by alcohol, or by my own hand, seemed to be the only escape. I was afraid to be awake and I was afraid to go to sleep. My days were spent feeling hung-over and my nights were filled with disturbing and frightening dreams. I lived with a constant feeling of doom pressing down on me.

Finally, having reached the end of myself, I prostrated myself on the floor of my home and cried out to God for forgiveness and deliverance from my miserable existence. I had called out to God many times before, mostly as a quick fix or fire insurance from hell. I would ask God for help and work to stay clean for a period of time, but then find myself right back at the bottle. This time, however, I was broken to the point that I was ready to do business with God on His terms, not mine, for the first time in my life. I had finally had enough.

While I was face down on the floor, I confessed every sin that I could remember. My body shook with emotion as the guilt of the last fourteen years came washing over me. As I confessed, flashbacks raced through my mind... drunken binges, immoral behavior, lies to everyone closest to me, greed, selfishness, and arrogance. I begged God to redeem my life, become my Lord and Master, and to fashion some sort of meaning out of my mess.

God answered me.

~

LET ME BE ABSOLUTELY CLEAR. I AM NO ONE SPECIAL. I AM not a doctor, a pastor, a theologian, a philosopher, or a counselor. I am a simple man with a simple life that was redeemed and renewed from the bondage of alcohol by the Lord Jesus Christ. I owe Him everything that I have and everything that I have yet to accomplish. This story is not meant to be a clinical study of alcoholism, nor is it a theological treatise or a self-help manual. This is just my own personal story of a life changed, an addiction broken, and hope restored by encountering a very real and personal God.

I know that there are literally hundreds of thousands, perhaps millions, of people across the world who are going through the same situation that I went through... people who are slaves to alcohol; people who are reaping the consequences of a life of alcohol abuse and sin; people who are dying from physical ailments due to their choices, but also from depression and hopelessness; people who have lost spouses, children, careers, and self-respect. It doesn't even matter if alcohol is the vice. People everywhere struggle with addictions and coping mechanisms, whether it is alcohol, pornography, drugs, gambling, or sex. No matter your condition, I want you to know that it is never too late to be redeemed and forgiven by God and to start afresh. As long as you have breath in your body, it is never too late.

It is my hope that anyone who is weighed down by the

burden of alcohol or other addictions will call out to God and be set free by His limitless power and grace. He forgave me and He will forgive you. As the Bible says in 2 Peter 3:9, *"The Lord is not slow in keeping his promise, as some understand slowness. Instead he is patient with you, not wanting anyone to perish, but everyone to come to repentance."* He wants you to come to Him. Please *let* Him forgive you and experience the true freedom and fulfillment of following Him. He is the only way to find true rest for your soul.

"Come to me, all you who are weary and burdened, and I will give you rest. Take my yoke upon you and learn from me, for I am gentle and humble in heart, and you will find rest for your souls. For my yoke is easy and my burden is light."

— Jesus Christ, Matthew 11:28-30

1

Drip, drip, drip. The sound was far away and cloaked in darkness. Drip, drip, drip. The sound was pressing in closer and slowly starting to deswirl the fog in my brain. My left eye opened just a crack. All I could see was white. White shower tiles. I struggled to make sense of the scene in front of me. Shower tiles? Where was I? My head was spinning in circles.

As I came-to, I realized I was lying on my back in my shower with my legs splayed up against the shower wall. I was fully dressed and covered in liquid. An empty rocks glass was broken on the tile floor beside me. The shower curtain and rod had fallen down around me. My head was pounding. I reached up and felt a painful lump on the back of my head, presumably where I had smacked it when I fell. The notion of having a concussion briefly crossed my mind before the haze overtook me again.

Beer and scotch. Lots of scotch. Slowly the events of the last few hours were coming back to me. I had gotten drunk. After three months of complete and hard-fought sobriety, I had gone on a drinking binge and ended up blacking out at the bottom of my shower with no memory of how I got there.

I grimaced as I realized I was laying in my own vomit and my clothes were soaked.

For the life of me, I couldn't remember why I'd gotten hammered in the first place. I had been on a roll. Three months of sobriety may as well have been a lifetime for me. The many weekends of resisting temptation, reading my Bible, not walking down the beer aisle at the store, faithfully attending church, and staying connected to others for accountability now seemed wasted. Wasted on a fleeting six pack of beer and a fifth of liquor.

My head was pulsing from the hangover and the fall against the tiles, but also from the realization. Why had I blown it? I shakily got to my feet and flipped on the faucet. The pounding water streamed down, washing the filth away, but the shame and disgust were impossible to wash down the drain.

I peeled off my soaked clothing and got dressed, crawling into bed more depressed than ever. Every time I thought I had conquered my addiction, I ended up right back where I started. *Maybe a drunk is all I'll ever be.* I glanced at the clock before I passed out; it was 3:07 a.m.

~

SIN HAS A COMPOUNDING EFFECT. NO ONE WAKES UP ONE DAY as a full-blown alcoholic. I certainly didn't. No one gets up in the morning, heads off to school or work and says, "You know, I think I'll wreck my life today." Instead, sin builds and builds over time, one small compromise after another.

My own personal series of compromises led me to a place of drunkenness and depression. By the time I was 34, I had earned a bachelor's degree in economics and a master's degree in business. However, if drinking could be taught, then I was far more accomplished in that area—a PhD with honors in drinking. Alcohol was dictating the trajectory of my life. I craved what alcohol did for me, but hated what drinking was doing *to* me. The bottom line is that alcohol had become my best friend and also my worst enemy. I was educated and accomplished, but I wanted to cut loose so badly and I felt that I needed the help of alcohol to do that. Once I began to drink, there was no limit to what I could get myself into.

Later as the drunkenness wore off and I began to detox, the shame and after-effects of alcohol would come crashing over me like one relentless ocean wave after another. The shame and remorse would last until I gave in to my next drinking binge and then the cycle would repeat.

Distractions helped, but they never provided a complete solution. I could temporarily throw myself into my job, or occupy my time with working out or spending time with a girlfriend or family. During military deployments, I could even go for six months at a time without alcohol. Alcohol was out of sight and out of mind. But eventually I would be home, sitting on my couch with nothing to do and no distractions to fall back on, and I would cave.

During those times, the only person to spend time with was myself. And I didn't like myself. I mostly drank to escape all thirty-plus years of struggles, mistakes, and shame, and as a result I couldn't abide spending time alone with myself. Rather than humbling myself and turning to God, I turned to alcohol to escape reality and provide a temporary fix.

I had reached a state of brokenness where I was completely consumed by my passions. The man in the mirror looked normal enough. Tall, muscular, brown hair, hazel eyes. I wore a uniform in service to my country. I appeared to have it all together. But it was an illusion. I had become very good at showing people around me what I wanted them to see. I could be a Marine Officer, a war veteran, an athlete, a musician, a historian, a reader, a chef, a golfer, a friend, a son, a brother, and a Christian. I could be whoever someone wanted me to be; anything but the *real* me. The real person behind the mask was weak. I doubted myself all the time. I tried to compensate for life's injustices in all the wrong ways. The real me was selfish, conniving, lustful, and immoral. The real me was someone who ended up in a shower stall soaking in my own vomit after a night of meaningless binge drinking. I was full of regrets, and I found it more and more difficult to shove away the realization of what drinking had done to me... what I had done to myself.

2

I was born in September of 1979 in the suburbs of Columbus, Ohio. My mother was a stay-at-home mom for me and my two younger brothers, and my father worked as an electrical engineer for a national telephone company. Some of my earliest memories were typical ones of a child from an average Midwestern family in the eighties— running around outside in the sunshine, riding bicycles with neighborhood children, playing soldier, building snowmen in the winter, and getting disciplined when I occasionally got out of line.

I attended kindergarten at a local church. I was born with a stutter, so I also went to speech therapy a few times a week in the hopes of being able to manage it and improve. My stutter aside, life seemed idyllic in those early years. We took family vacations, played games outside, spent time together in the evenings, and attended church together on Sunday mornings. There were barbecues and dinners we enjoyed as a family with other church members. One of my favorite memories from those days was when my dad would let me stay up late and watch Star Wars and Superman with him; I loved doing that together. Those early years were the best, but they didn't last.

By the time I was six years old, my parents were having marital problems and ended up filing for divorce just after my birthday that year. It was quite confusing and painful for me. I felt guilty, as if I had done something wrong. Up until that point, both my mother and father were very much involved in my life. Not having one of my parents live in the house was inconceivable. I wasn't old enough to realize that I was innocent and that my parents had split up for reasons far beyond my six-year-old ability to reason. Even though my brothers and I were still too young to fully grasp what had happened to our family, I knew that our way of life had changed forever.

After the divorce was final, we lived with our mom in an apartment in Reynoldsburg, a suburb of Columbus. Money was scarce in those days, with little income beyond child support and alimony, but we always had a roof over our heads, clothing to wear, and enough food to eat. To help make ends meet, my mother took up a paper route in the community delivering shopping ads and fliers for the local newspaper. We got to see our dad every other weekend and any other time that we wanted, but it just wasn't the same as having him in the same house with us.

After three years of living in the apartment, my mother remarried and moved us all to the state of Maine. We lived in a house on twenty-five acres of land situated in the middle of a vast forest outside the town of Unity in Waldo County. Our house was sparse and rustic, little more than a hunting cabin, and quite a change from what we were used to, but for three young boys, it was a dream come true. Cable TV didn't exist in those days and we didn't have video games. We had to create our own fun outside. Days were spent playing war, exploring the forest around us, riding our bicycles on the country roads, and floating paper boats on the creek at the foot of the hill.

I attended public school for my second-grade year, but afterwards my mother decided to home school my brothers and me. The population of rural Maine was so spread out that many families home schooled their children instead of dealing with the hassles of traveling many miles back and forth to the county school. There was a coalition of ten to fifteen home schooling families in our county, and we would get together at least twice a week for social and learning activities.

To supplement our schooling, my mom insisted that each of us boys learn to play an instrument as part of our education. I chose the piano and often played in recitals for our homeschool group and in church. Evenings were spent practicing our instruments and doing necessary chores around the house. The summers in Maine were terribly hot and humid, and the winters were bitterly cold. During an average winter, it sometimes snowed six feet in a night. Our house was heated by a wood burning stove, so we had to make sure that we never ran out of firewood. The consequences of firewood running low during the middle of winter were dire. Despite the hardships, I have good memories of life in the backwoods of Maine, although I was sad we lived so far away from our dad.

After four years of living in Maine, we packed up our lives again and my family returned to Lima, Ohio to be closer to our maternal grandparents. We had always been very close with them, especially my grandmother, and she doted on us boys. We moved into our grandparents' house while we searched for a place of our own. I was a twelve-year-old on the cusp of adolescence and I experienced the culture shock of leaving rural Maine and re-entering small-town Ohio.

All of a sudden, we were immersed in a way of life that was

foreign to us. Kids our age had nice clothes, new shoes, and crisp haircuts. They played sports and their families had nice houses and nice cars. They went to the movies on the weekends and took family vacations. Most of it seemed foreign to us now. When we lived in the backwoods of Maine, we didn't have to think about the latest fashions or what our hair and clothes looked like. We were used to a survivalist lifestyle and we did what we had to do to scrape by. We were used to playing our instruments and exploring the forest, not joining pick-up games of baseball with neighborhood kids or caring about the brand of shoes we wore. Coming back to Ohio was like moving to a different planet, but after a time, we began to feel accepted by the kids in our neighborhood and the people in our local church.

Instead of continuing to homeschool, my brothers and I started to attend Temple Christian School in Lima, Ohio. It was there that the cocoon in which we lived during the years in Maine truly began to unravel and a new world was exposed to us—a world of sports and social gatherings and girls. We naturally wanted to fit in with our friends and classmates. Except that by this point in my life, I noticed that patterns were already developed that made fitting in quite difficult.

All those formative years in Maine and the solitude spent through home schooling had formed the basis for the identity that I now had in Ohio. At thirteen years old, my identity was already wrapped up in the arts, music, and reading—things that are not exactly popular with the average kid. I didn't have a natural ability at sports and no organized leagues had been available during our time in Maine anyway, so the go-to activity of sports was not a way for me connect with others. I was shy and naturally introverted which led me to pursue solitary activities even more. And my stutter had also conditioned me to keep to myself and not venture out too much with others. This dynamic continued all throughout my teenage years and I constantly felt like an outsider.

MY HIGH SCHOOL CLASS WAS SMALL COMPARED TO OTHER schools in town, with only twenty-eight students. Most of my classmates had been attending since kindergarten so by the time I started at the school, there were already well-established groups. Within my class there were four social groups. We had the jocks, the pretty girls, the nerdy girls, and the "other guys."

There were four boys in the jock group. They were good-looking, popular, played basketball, baseball, and soccer, and were generally envied by all of the other boys. The jocks flirted with the girls, were smart enough to know most of the answers in class or at least were confident enough to always try to answer, and they generally seemed to be on the inside track to success.

The pretty girl group was made up of the athletes and the cheerleaders and of course, they were on best terms with the jocks. All the guys in my class had a crush on at least one of them, and the crushes rotated to different girls from year to year.

The nerdy girls group had some athletes, but they were mostly the intellectual type. The nerdy girls didn't seek attention and tended to keep to themselves. My group had the guys who were into video games, computers, science fiction, and reading J.R.R. Tolkien books.

One of the foundational, unwritten social rules of my school was that you couldn't change groups. Much like the Caste system, where you started at Temple Christian High School is where you stayed. Any attempt to change the system was met with resistance. Most of the time this was played out with criticism or mocking by a member of the desired social group. I certainly tried to make friends with some of the jocks or the pretty girls, but my efforts were nearly always rebuffed. Plus, my social inadequacies always got in the way.

I was extremely self-conscious about my stutter.

Sometimes a stutter can be reduced with therapy to where a person can speak with relatively few disfluencies, especially if the stutter is the result of trauma. I was not so lucky. My stutter was inherited from my paternal grandfather and speech therapy didn't seem to help me. It was very difficult to get through a sentence without tripping over the words or having them lock in my throat. This made me feel that I was damaged in some way. In fact, I can remember being bullied in the seventh grade and slammed into my locker by an upperclassman because he thought it was fun to ridicule a younger guy who couldn't talk straight.

Despite all this, I ended up with several acquaintances within the other groups at school. They seemed to like me on an individual level, even though I was never fully accepted as one of them. Even though we could converse or hang out one-on-one, they would never welcome me to the group or acknowledge me in public.

Like any other high school boy, I also had crushes on girls and I wanted to "go out," as we called it in the early 90s. The problem was that because of the unwritten social rules, re-enforced by my stutter, the pretty girls would not associate with me, let alone go on a date with me. In those days, the way to ask a girl out was to write her a sweet note, fold it up, stencil her name on it, slip it into her locker, and then wait for a response. Each of my attempts resulted in a "thanks for the offer but…" or just silence. I never had one date in all four years of high school.

The rejection stung. Dating and romance seemed to be something for other people but not for me. As my high school years progressed, I began to build an identity and belief structure around this pattern. I began to accept that I was a social pariah of sorts, someone who was always on the fringe of life. Because of my stutter and failures with girls in high school, I felt like a loner and a reject. My social standing seemed to be cheating me out of a normal life, and consequently, a void began to develop inside of me. I still had my few guy friends and church friends, but it wasn't the same as the widespread acceptance that I craved.

Up until this time, even with the negative reinforcement that I constantly received, I never once thought of turning to alcohol or drugs to find meaning or a new identity. I had been raised by Christian parents and was always in church, and those sorts of vices existed in an alternate universe to mine; instead, I just accepted my fate as an outsider. This created such a sadness in me as a teenager that I sank into a mild depression. I was afraid it would be like this for the rest of my life. I thought of myself as defective and even less deserving than others.

It was with this backdrop that I was exposed to alcohol for the first time.

3

When I was sixteen, I got a job at a local grocery store bagging groceries and bringing in carts from the parking lot. I felt good about this job because I was able to earn my own money and pay for the insurance and gas for my car and purchase other things that I wanted to buy. Many of my co-workers drank beer on weekends and at after-school events, but I didn't partake of alcohol myself for a few years more. Since my co-workers were between the ages of sixteen and eighteen, they couldn't buy alcohol for themselves, but they had older siblings or parents that would purchase it on their behalf. Even though my co-workers drank, and so did some of my friends, alcohol just wasn't something that I sought after.

It wasn't until the age of nineteen that I had my first drink. One of my best friends had gotten hold of a pint of high proof rum and we ended up doing shots at his house one weekend. It tasted horrible and it burned like fire. *Who in their right mind would want to drink this stuff?* I thought. My friend and I went shot for shot until the pint was gone. My head started spinning early on, but since I didn't have any experiences to compare it with, I didn't realize that I was getting drunk. The only reason I tried the rum in the first place was because it was something edgy, something I had not done before, and something that would shock people who knew me. I regretted the experience afterwards, and I was pretty sure that drinking alcohol in that manner wasn't something I would do again. Little did I know.

After I graduated from high school, I attended a year of community college. I studied business and pre-law and had aspirations of becoming a lawyer. I loved my classes about the law and government and felt that it was possibly the niche that I had been seeking. I could erase my high school years and forge a new identity as a lawyer; perhaps I could even become a politician. I was excited about the possibilities that lay ahead.

I almost never drank during that first year of college. I may have had a sip of beer or a single shot once in a great, great while, but that was it. At that time, I could have counted the times I had taken a drink on half the fingers of one hand. Most kids begin to drink heavily in college because they are away from their parents for the first time, but instead of drinking, I had a job teaching piano lessons at a local music studio. This job was fun for me and fit perfectly with my class schedule. I also joined a local gym, lost about forty pounds of kid flab and put on some serious muscle mass to match my 6'4" frame. I lived at home to keep expenses down and I was beginning to enjoy life as a young adult. There was some partying on the campus, but I was never a part of it. I was too busy teaching music and studying and working out.

As my freshman year of college ended, I began to feel restless. I felt that I needed to branch out and leave home and experience new things. My younger brother had spent the past year at a Christian college in Grand Rapids, Michigan. I thought perhaps that was where I needed to go next. It was only a few hours away from home and my brother was already attending school there. It seemed like a perfect solution. So, in the early spring of 2000, I applied and was accepted. I was thrilled about getting into the college and I began to make plans to move to Michigan for the fall semester.

I SHOWED UP TO MY NEW LIBERAL ARTS COLLEGE IN GRAND Rapids, Michigan, eager for my sophomore year of undergraduate studies. The campus is situated on the southeast side of Grand Rapids and I found it to be beautiful campus with ivy growing on the buildings, manicured lawns and walking paths, and more tulips than I had ever seen in one place before.

The college population numbered just under 4,500 students from across the fifty states as well as from Canada, Europe, and Africa. The school boasted sports teams, intramural clubs, and numerous student groups. Academics were stressed above all else and the course load demanded that students take their learning seriously. Because it was a Christian college, each student had to take a minimum of two theology courses. Chapel was offered every morning, but attendance was only mandatory for students taking certain classes. For students who felt a call to ministry, there was a graduate seminary on campus as well.

Underclassmen were required to live on campus in one of the six dormitory complexes. Each dorm was gender specific, but had two wings joined together in a common area. Each dorm had a dual name, one for the guys' wing and one for the girls. My dorm was named after some famous patrons of the campus. Upper classmen were afforded the opportunity to live in campus apartments or out in town.

For those students living in the dorms or apartments, the school imposed a code of conduct and a set of rules that were not to be broken. There was no smoking in the buildings or even within a certain distance of them and there was absolutely no alcohol on campus at any time. Living up to the college stereotype, students would break the rules from time to time and would have to face the consequences when they were caught. Most of the punishments were things like suspension from sports teams, a nominal fine, parental notification, and in the case of extreme violations, expulsion from resident life on campus.

Because of the strict code of conduct in place, students who had a desire to party or live on the wild side had to come up with all sorts of ways to indulge themselves outside of the boundaries of the campus.

There was a thriving underground party circuit at the college. The vast majority of the party scene was built around the students who lived off campus in the older part of Grand Rapids known as East Town. East Town was the oldest district of the city and reminiscent of early 20th century America. Many of the streets were still brick or cobblestone. Gas lamps illuminated every street corner, and quaint shops and dining establishments added to the charm of the district.

Because of the proximity to local colleges, most of the East Town homes had been converted to apartments which included an upstairs unit and a downstairs unit. If the house wasn't large enough to be converted into apartments, students could rent the house in its entirety. It was at these single unit houses where the underground party circuit thrived.

The parties were named after the street in East Town where the house was located: Carlton, Auburn, Wealthy, Diamond, and Fulton. The students who lived in these houses would put the word out around campus early in the week that there was going to be a large party at the house on Friday or Saturday night. Students circulated the news among their friends and began to work out the logistics of attending. The hosting students purchased several kegs of beer and assorted bottles of liquor and wine. When 9 p.m. on Friday or Saturday rolled around, a student would post up at the front door and charge party-goers $5 for a red Dixie cup and then they could drink all they wanted.

These kinds of parties were a big money maker for the hosts. There could be 50 to 100 people at a single house party. Students were willing to pay more than the $5 cover if the hosting students asked and there was never a shortage of students wanting to attend. Of course, there were never any questions of age or identification; money was the only ticket needed to get in. If a partier didn't like beer they could pay a little extra and get access to the liquor, or they had the option of bringing their own alcohol. If a student wanted to bring their own alcohol but was under the age of 21, they just needed someone one to purchase alcohol for them. That is where I came in.

I turned 21 two weeks after the start of the fall semester. Having just transferred from small town Ohio, I wanted to establish myself as someone with a decided cool factor. So, I let it be known that I would buy alcohol for underage students, especially girls. I had no lecherous intentions in buying for girls, but I wanted girls to like me more than the other guys, so I figured this would be my "in." Students approached me during the day on Friday and gave me money to buy the beer or liquor they wanted for that weekend. I even profited from the whole thing. The student handed me a $10 or $20, and I'd deliver the product, minus the change. It wasn't much, but after buying for 20 kids in a weekend, it began to add up.

Sometimes I made alcohol runs while the house parties were on-going. I even became known as "the guy who buys." I was just happy to be finally *needed* by people, even if the reason was less than desirable. Of course, I did more than just buy alcohol for students. I was also drinking more and more at these parties and found alcohol to be helping to loosen my natural shyness and social inhibitions. The deal with alcohol seemed like a win-win situation for me, even though I discovered it still carried some risks.

I remember one night I was at a house party on Fulton Street. A pretty blond named Becky had run out of beer and she and some of her friends wanted me to buy more for them. I was happy to do it and we all piled into her car and headed to the nearest 7-11. While we were out on the beer run, local cops came and busted the party. As with any illegal activity, getting caught is always a risk.

The local police were well aware of these house parties and knew just which houses to bust and what times they would be in full swing; the busts happened every weekend. A concerned citizen would call the police with an anonymous tip or a patrol car cruising the neighborhood would call it in and several squad cars would converge on the house and start shutting the party down. Students would run out the back and the hosts would be questioned thoroughly and all of the alcohol would be confiscated. The police couldn't do much because the drinking was on private property and most of the underage students would escape into the neighborhood. The fleeing students would rally somewhere close by at another house party or wait for the ruckus to die down and then come back.

As Becky and I drove back to Fulton Street after I bought the beer for her group, all we could see were flashing red and blue lights so she just kept on driving. I was moderately sober and had parked several blocks away, so she dropped me off at my car and she drove off with her friends and the alcohol. It was a close call.

I learned a valuable lesson that night. *Do not get caught.* Rather than deciding to make better choices and stop buying alcohol for minors, I just planned my purchasing a little more carefully. I knew if I got caught or if a student snitched that I was the one to buy, I could face academic repercussions. I could have lost my dorm privileges, faced academic suspension, have my parents notified, or a combination of all of them. But worse than that, I was afraid that I would lose my *cool* status, and I couldn't have that. I planned my purchasing a little smarter by only buying alcohol for people that I knew personally or by association. If a random student simply *heard* that I bought alcohol and approached me, there was no sale. It was just too risky.

~

AFTER MY SOPHOMORE YEAR ENDED, I WENT HOME TO OHIO to work for the summer. When I came back to Grand Rapids that fall for my junior year, I moved into an apartment across the street from campus. My brother lived with me, along with another friend attending the same school.

We had to get local jobs because we now had rent, food, and utility expenses. The jobs we had didn't pay us much money, little more than minimum wage, but it was enough to eke out an existence and still attend classes. We even supplemented our jobs by donating blood plasma twice a week.

We went to a donation center twice a week, went through the routine medical questionnaire, and then got hooked up to a plasma machine. A lab technician put a very large gauge needle into our arms, and the machine pumped out blood, spun the plasma out of it, and then returned the blood to our bodies. If we donated twice a week, we received $20 the first time and $30 the second time, all in cash. Donating plasma wasn't a glamorous way to earn extra money, but at fifty dollars a week in cash for minimal effort, we couldn't beat it.

Since I was now living off-campus, I became unplugged from my social network of house parties, and I stopped buying alcohol for minors and frequenting the weekend house parties in East Town. Instead, I chose to look elsewhere for alcohol and companionship.

During my junior year I frequented many of the clubs and local bars in Grand Rapids. The crowd was older and more sophisticated than the East Town house parties. Most of the clubs were downtown and upscale and guys in sloppy attire were not allowed inside the club. Girls dressed in sexy clothing and were always welcome. They put on their best clubbing outfits, spent extra time on their makeup, and then hit the clubs to dance and get guys to buy them drinks. If they were pretty, they could get into clubs even if they were underage. There was a rather seedy club near my college that was well-known for never carding girls.

Most of the reputable clubs had a cover charge, so an average night for me and my friends would involve several drinks at a smaller watering hole and then ending the night at one of the large clubs. The usual objective of going to the larger club wasn't to get drunk, but to pick up girls. This rarely happened for me because my ingrained self-consciousness still made me intimidated to flirt but drinking certainly helped take the edge off. Some of my friends who had a way with the ladies hooked up most of the time. But on a typical night, the girls were just content to dance, flaunt their bodies, and get free drinks from drunken frat boys. The girls knew how to play the game. You would think the guys would catch on eventually and stop trying, but the lure of a possible hookup meant the guys only tried harder and kept shelling out money for drinks.

It didn't take me long to develop a new party circuit with the bars and clubs in Grand Rapids. Live bands were featured on certain nights of the week and the bars had weekly drink specials in order to attract more business. Each bar would pick a certain night of the week and offer a free cover charge and cheap drinks. The bands would play several sets and the bar would then hold some sort of contest, usually a wet t-shirt contest. Once you learned the circuit, you could go out each night of the week on the cheap and drink to your heart's content. Most of my classes didn't start until 10 a.m. or later, so it was easy to stay out until 3 a.m. partying. I could get home and sleep it off, attend my classes for the day, go to my job until early evening, work out at the gym, and then hit the bar circuit. If I didn't have to work that evening, I went to the gym earlier and started partying sooner.

On the evenings that I didn't go out to party, I drank with my brother and roommate at our apartment. We drank quite often. My brother and our other roommate preferred beer while I was more of a liquor man. My drink of choice at the time was Castillo Rum. A bottle of this was only six dollars, and at that price, the rum fit well into my budget.

We typically didn't get falling-down drunk at the apartment; rather we preferred a constant and heavy buzz. We hosted cookouts on our porch and invited friends from campus to join us. Our apartment even became known as a get-away from campus life. Friends were always welcome and alcohol flowed in abundance. By the end of that year, we had accumulated over seventy empty bottles of liquor and hundreds upon hundreds of beer caps. I know this because we counted the bottles and beer caps when I helped my roommate move out later that summer. We stored them on top of the refrigerator because we wanted to see how much liquor we had consumed during the school year.

Even though I had stopped taking the risk of buying alcohol for minors, I started doing something even more foolish during my junior year—drinking and driving.

I braved the roads every time my friends and I went out on the town. There was never any question of having a designated driver or hailing a cab because I would drive us. In fact, I found that I enjoyed driving drunk. It was another way of living on the edge and doing something crazy and I was very good at it. I never had an accident or got pulled over. I never clipped my bumper or knocked over trash cans when pulling into a drive way. I had a little system of precautions. I took extra time to allow for decreased response time and cruise control became my best friend. I either drove the whole group back to a rally point, or if the guys lived close enough, I drove each of them back to their houses before heading home myself.

Sometimes I was so drunk that I woke up in my bed and could not remember how I got there because my last memory was having a great time at the bar. I'd call some of my friends and ask them what had happened. *Hey bro, you drove everybody home, don't you remember?* No, I did not, that was why I was asking! I would be shocked, but proud at the same time because I was able to get away with it. It was another feather in my cap and I wanted as many feathers as I could get in order to be *cool*. It didn't matter to me that I was breaking the law and taking chances. I dismissed all that. What mattered to me was social acceptance and having fun. I didn't care about the risks.

College life continued to be dominated by partying for the rest of my junior year and well into my senior year. As I started to think about graduating and the next phase of my life, I was suddenly struck with the realization that I didn't have all that much going for me. Even though I would be graduating with an economics degree and a minor in philosophy, my prospects for a job and a career were looking slim. I didn't have any internships lined up and my grades were well below 4.0 due to scraping by in my classes. I knew I needed to think beyond the next party on the horizon. A change in my life was needed… fast.

4

Towards the end of my senior year at college, I knew that I was headed for trouble. The partying and drinking were dominating my life. I was 23 years old and working two jobs, but for all of my work effort, I wasn't well-versed in professional life. The previous summer and academic year had been spent working in the mortgage industry and moonlighting at a men's business dress clothing store. I had several good months where I made money as a loan officer, but I found it to be an unstable way to make a living, at least with the abilities I had at the time.

I found myself choosing to either take care of my mortgage clients or attending class. I wasn't sure that I wanted to make the mortgage business my career, but I still wanted to be successful, so I ended up cutting a lot of classes and working all of the time, justifying it by telling myself that I needed the money and the mortgage business might be my future career anyway. The truth is that I didn't have the motivation to buckle down to both work and study. I was making an excuse to focus on work only so I would have the money and time to still lead the party lifestyle.

By the spring of my senior year, with the concern about

my grades and my future weighing heavily on me, I was looking to make a course correction. Fortunately, I found the direction I was seeking in the spring of 2003. The United States was still reeling from the 9/11 World Trade Center attacks and the military had boots on the ground in Iraq. Several acquaintances of mine were joining the military and they encouraged me to look into it for myself.

At first, I just laughed at them. Me? In the military? Not a chance. I was 65 pounds overweight thanks to my indulgent lifestyle, I had a stutter that plagued me, I had zero confidence in my abilities, and my self-discipline was sorely lacking. All that, my friends said, is exactly why I needed to join up. Tough as it was, I couldn't argue with their logic. I didn't have anything else more promising lined up. What could it hurt to do a little research?

I remember going down to the recruiting office that spring and talking to the different military services. I looked into each of the services, but early on I knew that I would end up choosing the United States Marine Corps. The Marine Corps had the "dress blues," after all. I thought it was the coolest-looking uniform that I had ever seen, with the emblazoned gold buttons, scarlet stripe down the trouser seam, sparkling sword at the side, and iconic white cover and gloves. The Marines pretty much had me at *hello.*

I talked with the Marine Corps recruiters for several hours about the opportunities available to me and what I would need to do. We hammered out a strategy for me to lose weight over the summer and attend boot camp in August.

The plan was for me to enlist in the Marine Corps Reserves initially, with an option to attend Officer's Candidate School later on to become a Marine officer once I completed my college degree. I needed to attend undergrad for a fifth year in order to take the final capstone course for my economics major, which was only offered in the spring semester. In the months leading up to that spring semester, I would complete Marine Corps basic training—boot camp— and the follow-on combat and occupational schools, and then I would check into my reserve unit. The Marine Corps Reserves allows for part-time military service, so this would work well since I needed to complete my undergrad schooling. While in the reserves, I would complete my college degree and report for service one weekend each month and two weeks in the summer. After receiving my degree the next spring, I would then be eligible for Officer's Candidate School and could become a commissioned Marine officer.

I was excited about my new path forward, feeling like the Marines would finally give me the discipline and confidence that I needed in order to make something of myself.

But before I could even fly to San Diego to attend basic training, I had to get myself in shape. I weighed 310 pounds and needed to weigh less than 245 pounds to even start basic training. I knew I couldn't lose the weight while living in Grand Rapids; there were too many distractions and the temptation to drink was too prevalent. In order to stay on schedule for my master plan, I had to leave for boot camp no later than the end of August.

So, I made the decision to quit the two jobs I held at the time and move back home to Ohio. That summer, I lived at my mother's house, paid her rent, and worked at a nearby factory unloading semi-truck after semi-truck of laundry detergent. It was long, hot, and miserable work, but it was full-time employment while I trained, trained, trained. I constantly monitored my weight loss progression against the days of summer ticking by. I absolutely had to stay on schedule. I ate salads, drank water, and ran ten miles a day. The weight began to melt off my body and after three months of hard training, I had lost nearly ninety pounds. I was lean and trim, ready for basic training. Mentally, I was motivated, with no second-guessing.

My mother drove me to Lansing, Michigan, to the military processing center on August 5, 2003. Recruits arrived for each branch of the military, including myself and others for the Marine Corps. The first day of processing was spent taking various medical and aptitude tests. At the end of the day, a bus arrived to transport all the Marine Corps applicants to a local hotel where we could get a good night's rest and then resume processing the next morning. Instead of going to bed early, nearly all the recruits hung out in the lobby, talked late into the night, or smoked cigarettes outside on the curb. Some of the kids acted tough, some were very quiet. I think everyone was nervous about what was in store for us.

The bus arrived the following morning at 5 a.m. and drove us back to the processing center for administrative paperwork that took the better part of the morning. Recruits couldn't get on a plane and simply "show up" at basic training. They had to have written orders for their military branch's basic training and arrive with their paperwork ready to go. The last event at the processing center before getting back on the bus and heading to the airport was taking the oath of enlistment.

I'll never forget it. There were about 40 of us in a room draped by red curtains. There was a dais in the front with each military service flag displayed behind a small lectern. A young Army captain walked in and called our group to attention. Then she told us to raise our right hands and repeat after her. We swore allegiance to the United States and promised to defend it against all enemies, both foreign and domestic. I felt proud as I lowered my right hand. After the ceremony, we picked up our paperwork and the Marine Corps recruits hopped on the appropriate bus for the ride to the airport.

I had a knot in my stomach during the entire flight. The recruiters had prepped me for Marine Corps basic training as much as they could, and I tried to review the information in my mind during the flight. They ran a program at the recruiting center in Grand Rapids called the Delayed Entry Program, for those enlistees who had a few months to wait before bootcamp. Kids were called "Poolees" and we met each week to learn Marine Corps knowledge, workout together, and have a general question and answer period. It was excellent preparation and I firmly believe I had a leg up on other kids arriving at basic training, but I would soon realize that nothing could truly prepare me for the reality of Marine Corps boot camp.

We started our final approach to the San Diego airport around 6 p.m. that same afternoon. Marine Corps Recruit Depot—MCRD—was adjacent to the airport grounds and from the air, we could see the physical training fields, obstacle courses, the 70-foot rappel tower, and the hallowed Parade Deck. And we saw platoons of recruits being trained by their drill instructors.

We touched down, deplaned, and made our way to the USO lounge. We bypassed the baggage claim because we were instructed to bring nothing to basic training other than the clothes on our backs and our paperwork. We settled in for a long wait in the USO lounge until the buses would arrive to take us onto the base.

The USO lounge was crowded with service members coming and going. We tried to blend in as best we could, but with our long hair and lack of military bearing, we easily stood out from the real service members. We chatted amongst ourselves and told each other how nervous we were. When the clock struck midnight, the doors suddenly opened up and a Marine Corps drill instructor came in and shouted at us. "Any of you going to boot camp, get outside right now!" There were about 75 of us in the room at the time and everyone froze for a second and then we all scrambled for the doors. I think the drill instructor managed to weave several curse words into that one shouted command, but my mind was in no condition to count just how many.

We lined up outside in front of several buses. After we climbed aboard, we were told to stay quiet and keep our heads in our lap for the duration of the bus ride. Even though the airport was right next to the base, the buses drove around for an hour or so to disorient us and then came to a stop outside the Recruit Reception Building on base.

As soon as the buses rolled to a stop and the door of my bus opened, another drill instructor raced up the steps onto the bus and screamed at the top of his lungs, "Sit up straight and get your eyeballs on me! You are now aboard Marine Corps Recruit Depot, San Diego, California, do you understand that!?" We all shouted back, "Yes, Sir!" He proceeded to lay down the law with some basic ground rules and then told us to "get off his bus right now." We raced off the bus as fast as we could and then all 75 of us took our positions on some painted yellow footprints that were arranged in platoon formation on the sidewalk.

Since we had arrived on a Wednesday night, recruits would be trickling in from around the country each day of the week and would be collected in holding platoons until enough recruits, usually around six platoons of 100 recruits, were present to begin training.

It was now about 1 a.m. For the next several hours, we stood in lines waiting to go to the next in-processing station. The first stop was the haircut. We filed in ten at a time, sat down in the waiting chairs and within a single minute, all of our hair was buzzed off. Then we were hustled over to an auditorium where we began to fill out the remainder of the in-processing paperwork. During this entire time, drill instructors and other Marines patrolled the hallways looking for recruits who were talking, not standing up straight, or not paying attention. When they found someone, they made an example of him. I learned very quickly to stand up straight, look directly ahead, and above all, keep my mouth shut.

By morning, everyone was starving. Our receiving drill instructor marched us all to the chow hall for breakfast and we sat down to eat. We had less than five minutes to eat an entire meal. Recruits who didn't eat fast didn't get to finish. Any recruit still eating when the drill instructor screamed that we were done got his food tray flipped and dumped all over himself. Next lesson learned—eat as fast as possible, but don't be the first one done. Once one recruit was done, the whole table was done. We quickly learned to eat at a fast and steady pace and finish together.

The next two days were spent marching from the barracks, to the chow hall, to medical and dental, and to the supply warehouse. We received about fifteen shots at medical, a quick tooth and mouth exam at dental, and then all of our uniforms and training gear at the supply warehouse. Everything was crammed into an oblong green canvas bag, called a sea bag, which we had to carry back to our barracks that afternoon. The next morning, we all had to run the Initial Strength Test, or IST. This test ensured that we had the basic physical fitness necessary to get through basic training. After the test, we went back to our barracks, showered off, and stood by to be sent off to our training platoons. Things were about to get real.

THE DAY YOU MEET THE DRILL INSTRUCTORS OF YOUR TRAINING platoon is called "Black Friday." It was about 10 a.m., and we marched from our receiving barracks across the base to our training barracks while carrying our sea bag, bedding, and paperwork. The long trek is specifically designed to make recruits drop their possessions and then everyone has to start over. By the time all 93 of us in the platoon got to our destination, without dropping anything, we were exhausted.

Once in the new barracks, we were assigned a bed, called a rack, along with a foot locker, and then told to gather in an area of our barracks called the quarter deck and sit down in even and orderly rows. A captain entered from the rear and the drill instructors entered from their office door and marched to the front of the platoon. The captain gave a motivational speech and told us what we could expect from him and his drill instructors. Once he was finished, the senior drill instructor stepped forward and emphatically introduced himself and his team of drill instructors. We all sat there wide-eyed and terrified. None of the drill instructors talked, they *screamed*. My mind raced with the thought that I had made a huge mistake. Did I really want to go through with this? Too late now. The Marine Corps owned me for four years, and I knew the fastest way out of basic training was to graduate on time. There was no real option of dropping out. Barring some kind of injury, the Marine Corps would keep recruits in the misery of basic training for as long as it took for them to finish.

When the senior drill instructor finished his speech, he turned the proceedings over to his next in charge, the drill instructor known as "the heavy". He gave us an orientation for how things would be done from there on out. Every item was referred to with naval terminology. Windows were now portholes. Showers were called rain trees. Walls were now bulkheads. Everything he said was followed with a loud, "Do you understand that?!" But he would say it so fast that it came out as "you unnerstanat!?" To which we all shouted "YES, SIR!" He told us to train hard and above all else, to never give up, to never quit. If we would stay the course, we too would be United States Marines.

After shouting these things at us, he paused and then screamed for us to get up from our seated positions on the floor and "get on line" in front of our footlockers. Getting on line meant standing on an imaginary line in front of our footlockers, at the foot of our racks. It was a way for the drill instructors to maintain visual accountability of every recruit at once.

The senior drill instructor finished observing his "heavy" bark out instructions to us. Satisfied with the performance, he went back into his office while his team of three drill instructors tore into us with a holy fury. Chaos and stress abounded. The drill instructors' sole mission that morning was to disorient, terrify, stress, and confuse us. They yelled instructions and had us screaming responses back at them so loud that we lost our voices after the first hour. We could hardly put two words together. New terminology was thrown at us, some of it the military terms for things, but other things meant to disorient us.

We grasped onto the proper responses for things as quickly as we could. When the drill instructors yelled, "Eyeballs!" meaning to look at them, we learned to yell back, "Click!" and we better be looking. The command of "Ears!" was answered by "Open, Sir!" That meant the drill instructors needed us to listen to something important. "Zero!" meant that we were supposed to freeze in the moment, as in do not even blink, no matter what position we were in at the time. The drill instructors could easily control the platoon with these three simple commands. They would shout these commands ten times in a row just to irritate us because we'd have to respond each time. There was no slacking off allowed in terms of volume, either. The drill instructors would yell at us to "sound off with some volume and intensity!" To emphasize the point, one of them spat out, "You will not sing Christmas carols to me in my bootcamp, you unnerstanat?!" For certain, none of us felt ourselves to be in any kind of festive mood as we screamed back the proper responses as ordered.

Throughout that first long day of Black Friday, the drill instructors put us through hours of pointless exercises, just because they could. They had us running from one end of the squad bay to the other, again and again. After we were exhausted, we'd have to put on our sweat suits, then our camouflage uniforms ("cammies"), then our water proof coats, wrap our blankets around our necks, and do it all over again while trying not to slip and slide in all the sweat on the floor. They had us dump our sea bags and the contents of our foot lockers and kick all the clothes and gear around into a huge pile and then low crawl through it. Then they'd give us 30 seconds to pick it all up, put it back in our sea bags and foot lockers, get on line, and do it all over again. They had us sweating and shaking, and this continued on for the rest of the day.

At the end of the day we were told to undress and get in the showers for hygiene time. I thought that maybe I'd finally get a little reprieve from the yelling and stress, but the drill instructors charged right into the showers with us in full uniform and started showering us together "by the numbers." That meant a countdown for every movement. The drill instructor screamed, "Left arm, wash it right now! 10, 9, 8, 7…2, and 1, you're done right now!" Then it was on to the right arm, then the left leg, and so forth and then we were shoved out of the showers still covered in soap and shampoo. When we finally collapsed in our racks that night to sleep, I was thoroughly convinced that I'd made a terrible mistake in joining the Marine Corps. Basic training was 13 weeks but as far as I was concerned, it seemed as if 13 lifetimes stretched endlessly ahead of me.

BASIC TRAINING WAS DIVIDED INTO THREE PHASES, EACH ONE of them a month long. The first phase was pure indoctrination into the Marine Corps world. Each day began at 5 a.m. and ended at 9 p.m. We had three to four classes each day where we learned Marine Corps history, proper wear and care of our uniforms, weapon systems, ethics and codes of conduct, medical triage, and customs and courtesies. We had physical training—PT—and martial arts training each day. We practiced drilling and marching with our rifles for hours each day.

Everything was new to us.

We had to memorize the new terminology that was forced on us starting day one. A pen was no longer a pen, it was an "ink stick." The stairs were no longer stairs, they were "ladder wells." On the rare occasion that a recruit was allowed to speak, he had to refer to himself in the third person, never as "I" or "me." Individual identity was no longer allowed.

We had to learn the military rank structure and address officers with the title of *Sir*. There were no calendars, no clocks, and no watches. The only way to tell time was by meals and counting the days between church services on Sunday. The goal was total disorientation and separation from our former lives and identities, with the intention of putting us back together as a functional team. Every waking moment of every day, the drill instructors were on us, always yelling. There was not a single moment unaccounted for each and every day. I thought that maybe the drill instructors would ease up after the first several days, but the pressure only seemed to increase.

There was not one moment of peace. Church services provided the only escape from the drill instructors. Services were optional, but nearly every recruit attended. This was the one place on the base that drill instructors were not allowed. The services lasted about three hours and I attended each week. The only other alternative was to stay in the barracks under the constant eyes of the drill instructors.

Phase One of basic training ended with the Initial Drill competition. My training company was made up of six training platoons, and each platoon competed against each other in a choreographed drill routine. The platoon that executed the movements on the drill card with the least mistakes was declared the winner. It goes without saying that the instructors were merciless in their preparation of the drills leading up to the actual competition day.

The morning of the competition dawned bright and clear. We put on our cleanest uniforms, polished our weapons, and marched out to the Parade Deck. We did not have the entire routine memorized, but the senior drill instructor had the movements on a drill card and called out the commands in sequence. I was nervous about how we would perform, but once the initial jitters passed, I thought that we did very well. All 93 of us moved together as one person. I imagined that we looked good from the reviewing stands.

After the competition, we marched back to our squad bay and stood by while the results were compiled. I stood in front of my footlocker and breathed a sigh of relief as my platoon, number 1022 of Delta Company, was called out as the Initial Drill winner. I could then hear the five other platoons above, below, and across the hallway in their own squad bays getting yelled at and punished mercilessly by their drill instructors.

I knew the likely punishments. Recruits would be bundled up in their uniforms, blankets, and waterproof ponchos, and ordered to carry their sea bags on their backs. Then the drill instructors would keep the recruits running back and forth across the squad bay, doing pushups and jumping jacks, dumping the contents of their foot lockers and then low-crawling on the concrete, all of this for hours and hours until the recruits were hot and sweaty messes. All of us in the winning platoon breathed a sigh of relief because we knew it was miserable for the other five losing platoons that day.

The day after the Initial Drill competition, we began the move to Camp Pendleton to begin Phase Two of basic training. We packed up our squad bay and loaded everything into a large semi-truck, then boarded buses and headed north. We arrived at Camp Pendleton two hours later and drove to

Edson Range, the space where recruits lived and trained. Of course, the stress was not going to ease up. The drill instructors had to shake us up a little so that we wouldn't forget we were still in basic training.

I remember being ordered to run around a large dirt field with my sea bag on my back and sweating through my uniform until I was drenched. One of the drill instructors known as the "kill hat" had taken an unfortunate liking to me and some of the other recruits, and he decided to make us into "sugar cookies." We were ordered to drop our sea bags and get down on our hands and knees so the drill instructor could slather thick goops of sunscreen all over our heads, neck, and faces. We then had to roll around in the sand so that it stuck to our exposed skin. Then it was back to running with our full sea bags, our faces and necks now coated in gritty sand. The sunscreen ran into my eyes and stung, mingled with the sweat, and the sand got everywhere. It was miserable. There was no luxury of a long, hot shower to get clean. Instead, I was still trying to get rid of the remnants of sand several days later during the rapid-fire group shower sessions.

Once the drill instructors completed their fun and games at our expense, we started Grass Week. This was a relatively calm period where we learned the fundamentals of the M16A2 service rifle and how to properly care for the weapon and fire it. We spent a lot of time on our bellies in the grass as we practiced our aim. Although the instruction was still intense, we had a reprieve from the typical stress and yelling as we focused on handling our weapons.

Firing Week followed, where we put the fundamentals from Grass Week to good use and practiced a course of fire each day. Final qualifications took place on the Friday that week. I shot fairly well and earned a sharpshooter's badge. The third week was Field Week. We went on forced hikes in the mountains of Camp Pendleton and learned about land navigation and survival in the field. I rather enjoyed this part of basic training, if one can enjoy any part of bootcamp, because it seemed we were learning practical things instead of getting screamed at for incorrect drill routines.

Field Week ended with us having to endure the gas chamber. Each of us was fitted with a gas mask and taken into a concrete bunker and told to stand against the walls. A Nuclear, Biological, and Chemical Marine—or NBC—placed a tablet of CS gas, one of the most common tear gases, on a burner and lit the fuse. We could see the green CS gas swirling and permeating the room. Seeing the green mist swirl and spread was a little unnerving, but I was able to stay calm and breathe through my mask like we were taught. Panic got the better of many recruits and they pulled their masks off in an attempt to breathe. Big mistake. Inhaling CS gas isn't at all fatal, but it is quite painful and irritating to the eyes and skin.

Naturally, the drill instructors were right there to mess with the recruits that panicked. Some poor kid would be rubbing his eyes, hacking and doubled over in pain, and the drill instructors would be right there with him screaming at him to do jumping jacks and pushups. All the exercise just made the recruit inhale more of the gas.

The most difficult part of the gas chamber was learning to don and clear the mask. On command, we were told to take our masks off, wait 30 seconds, then put the masks back on and clear the canister so we could breathe. If executed properly, there was no trouble at all. If a recruit panicked and opened his eyes or breathed in, pain ensued due to the exposure. After what seemed like hours, but really was no more than 10 minutes, we were all ushered out of the gas chamber and into the open air to breathe deeply and get some relief.

The final week of Phase Two was The Crucible, an exhausting 56-hour event that put to use all of the field skills that we had just learned. We only received two meals and four hours of sleep during the entire event, mimicking the elements that we might have to endure to survive in actual combat. We marched through the night, went on simulated assault missions that attacked fictional enemy positions, negotiated combat courses and obstacle courses, received training in hand-to-hand combat, and received lessons in leadership from our drill instructors.

The last few difficult hours of The Crucible were spent hiking up The Reaper, a dangerously steep mountain overlooking Camp Pendleton. Our bodies ached, but we climbed and trudged our way to the top and it felt so good to finally reach the summit. We savored the views that spanned for nearly 50 miles in all directions on that sunny clear-skied day. The Pacific Ocean stretched out in endless blue to the west and we could see the enormous Camp Pendleton below us, looking small now. Our drill instructors congratulated us on a job well done and actually told us they were proud of us. Then we formed up and began the 10-mile hike back to our barracks.

By the time we arrived back at the barracks our feet were bruised and bloodied and our bodies felt battered, but we were proud to have conquered The Crucible. The drill instructors marched us to the chow hall and we enjoyed a large buffet-style feast. I don't think any meal to this day has tasted quite so wonderful.

Phase Two ended and we packed up our squad bay, boarded the buses, and drove two hours south back to MCRD San Diego. Our drill instructors didn't mess with us after arriving this time. Instead, we were ushered into our squad bays, calm and orderly, and we started cleaning the area and getting ourselves ready to begin Phase Three.

Phase Three consisted of tests of the various things we'd learned in the previous two phases. We went through a final knowledge test, medical triage test, final physical fitness test, swim qualifications, martial arts testing, and more drilling in preparation for the upcoming Final Drill competition. During this last month, we also spent a week in working parties around the base performing cleanup and maintenance activities. Our drill instructors were not present during the day. It was such a blessed relief to have some time to ourselves, even if the days were spent working. We were still under watchful eyes, however. If a recruit acted out of line, his drill instructors were promptly notified and the recruit was punished, so we stayed on guard.

The last week of basic training began with the Final Drill competition on Monday. This time, my platoon got second place and we paid for the loss severely. Our senior drill instructor came out of his office with thunderclouds cracking across his face.

He ordered all of us to get outside in front of our barracks and then he marched us straight to the sandy area of the physical fitness fields and proceeded to make us roll around in the sand and workout in the heat for an hour. The sand got everywhere. Sand was still falling off us as we marched back to the barracks and up the stairs to our squad bay. This only made our barracks dirty, so the drill instructors had fun making us clean it all up.

Tuesday and Wednesday of that final week were spent doing administrative paperwork as we eagerly anticipated the events to take place on Thursday, also known as Family Day. This was the long-awaited day when our families would arrive to watch us march out to the Parade Deck to receive our Eagle, Globe, and Anchor devices. This iconic symbol of the Marine Corps would mean that we were now Marines.

I still remember the day vividly. More than a few recruits and even a few hardened drill instructors choked up with emotion during the ceremony. Passing on the Eagle, Globe, and Anchor devices and making new Marines is a sacred honor and one that the drill instructors hold with great reverence. My family sat in the bleachers and looked on as I was officially made a United States Marine. It was a moment of wonder and pride for me as I reflected on the history, tradition, and honor of being inducted into such a hallowed institution.

Once the ceremony was over, the drill instructors marched us back to our squad bays, gave us a few instructions about proper behavior, and then allowed us to leave the squad bay and find our families on the Parade Deck. I quickly found my family and after all the hugs and congratulations, I gave them a tour of the base.

My family couldn't believe how different I looked. I had started my journey six months before basic training weighing 310 pounds and had drastically lost weight to get to basic training. Now I was wearing a United States Marine Corps uniform and was even leaner after 13 weeks of basic training, with muscles as a bonus. I didn't even look like the same person! Beyond just looks, my bearing and demeanor had completely changed. The timid guy who always hung back in the crowd and was afraid to speak up was gone. The drill instructors had burned those weaknesses out of me with the fire of Marine Corp toughness and discipline.

My family and I enjoyed a nice luncheon hosted at the Officer's Club on base and then we spent the rest of the afternoon talking and relaxing. I regaled my family with stories of the hardships and accomplishments over the last several weeks, but I had to return to the barracks by 5 p.m. All of us worked late into the evening cleaning the squad bay, preparing our uniforms, and packing our sea bags and foot lockers. We staged everything in the center of the squad bay, hit the showers, and then crawled into our racks.

Morning arrived and we lined up in front of our barracks and then stepped off to breakfast. We inhaled our food, marched back to the barracks, and spent the next few hours getting our gear staged outside, uniforms on, and our black patent leather shoes polished to a mirror shine. Around 11 a.m., we formed up outside to wait for our senior drill instructor. When he arrived, he stepped in front of the platoon and ordered us to "Right face! Forward, March!" And with that, we were off to the Parade Deck.

Our families were in attendance to see us graduate. We went through a choreographed ceremony that ended with the entire Delta Company marching past the reviewing booth where the general officers sat. When we finally stopped, our senior drill instructor gave the command to right face and we executed the command flawlessly. We turned to the right and clicked our heels into place. Then the commanding general gave the command to dismiss the platoons from basic training. Our senior drill instructor shouted in response, "Platoon 1022, you are dismissed from basic training. Fall out!" As abruptly as basic training had begun three months before, it was over with one command. But it felt incredible.

5

After graduation, I was given a ten-day period of leave. I flew home to Ohio with my family and visited people at church and then drove up to Grand Rapids to visit my school friends. No one recognized me at first; I looked that different. After months away to prep for basic training and then the months of basic training itself, I was tall, lean, and muscled with the Marine haircut and a newfound sense of accomplishment and confidence. People enjoyed hearing about basic training and seeing my uniforms.

After the ten days came to an end, I flew back to San Diego and boarded a bus to Marine Combat Training at Camp Pendleton, California. This is a three-week school that is designed to teach new Marines more in-depth combat and survival tactics. We spent every day outside in the mountains of California learning land navigation, small unit tactics, hand-to-hand combat, and advanced survival strategies.

After Marine Combat Training, I flew back to the east coast and reported to Camp Johnson in Jacksonville, North Carolina for my specific occupational training. My chosen occupational field was supply chain management, and I spent the next five weeks learning how to handle logistics for the

Marine Corps. We lived on base in dormitory-like barracks and it was a pleasant experience after the hardships of basic training. I drank a little bit here and there, but I was still reveling in my new Marine status and I wasn't looking to get drunk. I graduated the Basic Marine Warehouseman's Course with honors for my occupational training and was meritoriously promoted to Lance Corporal.

Now that the first stage of my Marine training was complete, I needed to get back to Michigan to check in with my reserve unit and get back to finishing college. Several months before, I had arranged to live with one of my school friends in an apartment house in East Town. This was the scene of so much partying during my sophomore year, when I was also buying drinks for all the underage students, but I told myself to keep it together, buckle down, and finish school. Having my degree in-hand would allow me to get to Officer's Candidate School which was my next driving goal.

My final semester at college started in February of 2004 with one important last class to go—my economics capstone course. I was now in the Marine Corps Reserves and my reserve commitment suited my schedule well. The reserves only required one weekend a month and two weeks in the summer. This afforded me the opportunity to live in both worlds at the same time, but it also convinced me even more that an active duty Marine Corps career was what I wanted. Finishing my degree would let me embark on the next phase of becoming a Marine officer.

The discipline that was hammered into me at basic training was just what I needed to finish strong at school. I applied the discipline and tenacity that I had learned in basic training to my studies. My grade point average improved to a 3.2, I never cut class, and I was able to hold down a night job as a security guard at a local factory in town. During the months while I completed my capstone course, I didn't fall back into the prolific drinking and partying like I had before the Marines. I still drank and I occasionally went out on the town, but my focus was on finishing school and doing well in my reserve unit. I graduated with my bachelors degree in May of 2004 and began to put together my officer candidate package.

Now that school was finally over, I continued to live in East Town with my friend and work nights as a security guard. I maintained my physical fitness, but without the demands of school I found myself slipping back into my old ways and filling up empty nights with alcohol and going to bars. The money I made as a security guard wasn't great, but supplemented with my Marine Corps reserves pay, I made enough to pay my rent, my car payment, food, and of course, buy alcohol. I found myself drinking more and more with my roommate. We'd run out of alcohol so I was frequently walking down to the grocery store just one block away from the house to restock.

For some reason, unlike my studies, after graduation I didn't connect the discipline of the Marine Corps with cleaning up my destructive personal habits. The compelling drive to finish school had kept me from drinking and partying for a time, but now extra time on my hands made it easy to fall back into my old ways. About the only thing I quit was my propensity to drive after drinking. That was now a no-brainer. The Marine Corps would punish me severely if I got a DUI. My ambition was to be a Marine officer and a DUI would be a sure-fire way to end that dream. Besides, many of the bars in East Town were within walking distance of our house, so we just walked.

My roommate was something of a self-professed alcoholic himself, so he and I frequented the bars in town often. We became quite fond of one Irish pub named Mulroney's. It was little more than a dive bar frequented by college students and other young adults. I liked the atmosphere and best of all, the drinks were super cheap. Ten dollars was more than enough to get drunk at Mulroney's if you stopped by on the night with specials.

Besides the ease of drinking, I liked the place because mixing it up with the underclassmen made me feel important. Here they were, still early in their college career, and I had not only graduated with my degree, but I was also a United States Marine. I made sure everyone knew I was a Marine.

I was rightly proud to be a Marine, but after so many years of feeling like I didn't measure up, it was also the way to make myself feel superior to everyone around me. For the first time in my life, I had something that other people didn't. I was still shy when it came to approaching girls, but I would find my courage when they approached me instead. I discovered that my distinctive haircut, lean physique, and new-found personal confidence now led women to come over and ask me with interest if I was in the military. Once the ice was broken, it was easy to talk to girls. My old identity was gone. Now I had a new one, an identity as a Marine.

When my roommate and I were not drinking at Mulroney's pub or some other bar, we were drinking in our apartment or with the guys that lived in the apartment below us. Our house had a rather large front porch and we often hosted house parties. Our parties were nothing on the scale of the East Town house parties that I attended as a sophomore, but they were still wild. In fact, we hosted a costume party for Halloween that year. I toyed with the idea of wearing my dress uniform to the party but I had the good sense to leave my expensive uniforms in the closet. Instead I wore a ridiculous leopard print blazer, a pinstriped shirt, and a crazy hat to match the crazy night of drinking that followed. Lucky for us, the police never came to bust our party even though we were loud enough to warrant police attention.

Drinking had become a way of life again, but I made excuses in my mind. Countless times, I remember getting drunk on our front porch and leaving bottles and beer cans and cigarette butts all over the place. There were homeless people living on the streets of East Town and they came by like clockwork to clean up the bottles and cans on our porch in order to collect the 5-cent refund that Michigan offered. I found this to be rather fortunate and even charitable of myself. Here I was able to drink and carouse, and someone else cleaned up the mess and benefitted themselves as well. In a twisted way, I believed I was doing the homeless a service.

Drinking was how I marked time while waiting on my Marine officer candidate package to be accepted, and I laughed off any drinking-induced escapades. I remember there were some ratty old recliners on the porch and my roommate and I would fall asleep in them after drinking all night and wake up outside covered with dew. We'd simply laugh and head inside to our respective bedrooms to get some sleep. In my mind, drinking was still no big deal and my intended career path as a Marine was unfolding on course.

6

My Marine officer candidate package was accepted in the fall of 2004, and I received orders to report to Officer Candidate School at Marine Corps Base Quantico in January of 2005. I was excited for the opportunity to become an officer and enthusiastically began the process of closing out my life in Grand Rapids. I sold my furniture, received my final paycheck from my security guard job, packed up my belongings, and headed back to Ohio a week before Christmas for some family time. I stayed sober that holiday season, more so out of respect for the journey I was about to embark upon, rather than any sense of moral conviction.

I was required to report to Officer Candidate School on January 15, 2005. I arranged to drive to Quantico, Virginia with another candidate who would be attending Officer Candidate School with me.

Jason and I left at the crack of dawn on the morning of the 15th. It was very cold with snow on the ground, and the wind whipped the snow in swirling circles through the air. He pulled into our driveway at 5 a.m. I said goodbye to my mom and hugged her, tossed an overnight bag into the backseat, grabbed my orders, and we took off on the eight-hour drive east. Jason had no prior military training so he was more than a little curious and nervous about what was going to happen. I couldn't speak for the officer side of things, but I was certain the events would unfold in a similar fashion to enlisted basic training. I told him everything I knew about the Marine Corps, basic training, drill instructors, and how the general process worked. As the drive wore on, we swapped stories from college and our previous lives and began to build a firm friendship.

We arrived at Quantico in the early afternoon. A knot had been forming in my stomach from the time we crossed over the Maryland state line into Virginia, and as we passed through the main gate of Quantico, that knot tripled in size. I had never been to Quantico before, but base personnel had put signs along the road directing officer candidates to the right place.

The Officer Candidate School grounds were located at the farthest point from the main gate, right along the Potomac River. We followed the signs to the student parking lot and pulled into an empty space, looked at each other, and took a deep breath. Things were about to get real. We grabbed our respective bags, shook hands, and headed towards the administration building. It was so cold outside that our breath seemed to turn to ice before it even left our bodies.

I vividly remember shouldering my bag across the school grounds through a bitter wind and a lightly falling snow. The temperature had dropped to 10 degrees and I pondered grimly what life would be like for the next ten weeks in the bitter cold. Since I had some experience with Marine Corps training techniques by this point, I knew that most of our training was going to be outside, some of it in the frigid water, and nearly all of it without the apparent luxury of protective warming layers.

Although the thought made me inwardly grimace, I also

felt a certain sense of pride that Marine Corps training is one of the most intense and difficult training programs anywhere. Marines are expected to gut it out in the most miserable of conditions, and thus, the training environment for recruits and candidates is often orchestrated to be miserable in order to prepare for the rigors of combat. Being soaked and drilling outside in the freezing wind would not be pleasant in the least, but I was ready for the challenge. I had already survived basic training after all; I hoped that my candidacy for the officer program would be just as successful.

As Jason and I reached the administration building, the doors were opened by some enlisted Marines and we were rudely told to shut up and get in a line of candidates that had been formed against the back wall of the foyer. Welcome to Officer Candidate School. Jason looked pretty wild-eyed but I snapped back into basic training mode and did what I was told.

Our paperwork was processed and we were moved along the line and out the back door and into a neighboring warehouse that served as a classroom. Inside were folding tables arranged in neat and even rows; there must have been enough space for 500 candidates, even though we numbered far less than that. The instructors organized us by platoons and we filed off to our seats and stared straight ahead. We waited for what seemed like forever. As the afternoon hours ticked by into the evening, we were finally told to remove our shirts and put on the green Marine Corps t-shirt. We still had our civilian pants, but our shirts and coats were stored away in backpacks. Then we sat there some more, staring straight ahead and not saying anything. We were now into the early morning hours.

After all those hours of waiting, we were finally given a reprieve from the hard seats and the boredom of sitting awake all night with no interaction. We were issued a thin, waterproof coat called a Gortex and then told to line up outside so that we could all march to the chow hall for breakfast. The chow hall was situated on the banks of the Potomac river, and at that early hour of 5 a.m., the wind screaming off the river tore through our ranks and made us shiver down to the bone as we marched in the dark.

Just at the point that we could no longer stand the biting cold, we were allowed to go inside the chow hall and get warm. Such relief! And unlike basic training where they yelled at us the entire time, we were given 15 minutes to eat in relative peace.

During the next two days we received our haircuts, basic gear issue, and our consumable supplies. We also ran the physical fitness test to see which candidates were physically ready to start training. It wasn't enough to pass this test. We had to pass it with a first-class score. Anything less would result in being expelled and sent home.

I had never run a physical fitness test in such cold. When I jumped up on the pull-up bars the freezing steel sent chills down my arms and locked them out which made it much tougher to perform the repetitions. I looked around and noticed the other 250 candidates were not fairing any better than me, so I took a little comfort in that. Fortunately, after the scores were tallied, I scored high enough to begin training.

Since we took the physical fitness test on Friday morning, I predicted that if Officer Candidate School was anything like basic training, I could expect a "Black Friday" type event coming later that day. I wasn't disappointed.

After lunch we marched back to the warehouse/classroom and filed into our respective platoon sections. I was in the second platoon and our spot was up near the front on the right side of the room. The commanding officer, a full bird colonel, took his place in the front and spoke to us for several minutes about what we could expect and what would be required of us. So far so good. Then he introduced the captains who were the instructor platoon commanders, and finally he introduced the drill instructors. I knew what was coming next.

The platoon commanders moved down the center of the aisle and the drill instructors moved along the perimeter of the wall, forming a complete circle around the room. The colonel raised his voice and said, "Platoon Commanders, take charge of your candidates and carry out the plan of the day!"

All restraint broke loose at that point. The drill instructors moved in with a vengeance and tables and chairs started flying and tipping over. The shouting and screaming increased in volume as the stress levels rose. I can't tell you why, but I found myself rather enjoying the commotion and stress. It was a deja vu moment. It wasn't as intense as basic training, probably because I had expected it, so I just did what I was told and moved as fast as I could. I saw the fear and chaos in the eyes of my non-Marine candidates, though. For them, it was the first time they had experienced the drill instructors, and they had absolutely no clue what was going on.

As ordered, we raced outside of the classroom, grabbed our sea bags of supplies, and ran to the Parade Deck located adjacent to our classroom. The drill instructors chased us and screamed the entire time. "Faster right now! Get in platoon formation right now!" We stumbled into some sort of platoon formation and tried to stand at attention while the snow and wind whipped around us. The drill instructors got us organized and then we filed into the barracks by platoon and took up positions "on line" in front of our new footlockers in our respective platoon squad bays. Once on line, the drill instructors ran up and down the wide aisle between the racks and footlockers, an area called the drill instructor highway, and continued to increase the stress and screaming.

The afternoon unfolded just like that first day of enlisted basic training, only on a less severe scale. I came to find out that the goal of Officer Candidate School was not to tear away the individual in exchange for a well-functioning unit, but to create leaders who could think and give commands under stress. The different goal for officer candidates required a different kind of training.

As Officer Candidate School got underway, I evaluated it against my experience during enlisted basic training. I found Officer Candidate School to be just as hard, only in a different way. Basic training was mentally difficult because of the mind games, the seemingly pointless exercises, the drill instructors that constantly screamed, and the bevy of new challenges. However, Officer Candidate School was exponentially more difficult in terms of leadership and physical fitness.

Since I was already a Marine, the history, drills, uniforms, and tactics were easy for me. In fact, my status as a "prior" Marine made me a go-to guy right from the start. I knew how to take care of my gear, and I was well-versed ahead of time as to what the instructors were looking for in leadership evaluations. I knew how the "games" were played. The candidates without any prior Marine Corps experience were flying blind. Those of us with prior experience made it our mission to help out the guys that had none.

I noticed early on that unlike the drill instructors at basic training, the drill instructors at Officer Candidate School were not there to constantly scream, break down, and remold the candidates. Instead, their mission was to train and evaluate. Boot camp was all about creating basic enlisted Marines that would instantly respond to orders. Now as potential officers, we were being evaluated on our ability to think through stressful situations and come up with plans that were executable. Our new drill instructors were not so much mean as indifferent and cold. They still yelled of course, but their general attitude was one of observation and screening. They constantly put us into situations where we had to quickly assess a set of circumstances, make a decision, and then lead our peers through the exercise. And all the while the instructors were there, watching and writing comments on their clipboards. It added a whole new level of stress. Would I measure up? Did I perform well enough on that last exercise? Was something being evaluated that wasn't even on my radar?

The entire ten-week program was broken down into sections, each with a major milestone event to complete before moving on to the next one. The first of these milestones took place at the end of the first four weeks and was called the Small Unit Leadership Evaluation #1 event, or SULE 1.

The exercise had each platoon broken down into "fire-teams," or essentially teams of four candidates. Each team had a required number of tasks to complete within a set amount of time. Each task required a leader and we rotated leadership positions. Each task was located a mile or so apart, so we were running from task to task.

When it came to my turn to lead, my task was organizing my team into a casualty evacuation team where we had to drag a 200-pound mannequin through the woods and down a steep grade to the lake shore, all while under notional enemy fire. The instructors imposed difficult constraints like only two candidates could touch the mannequin at a time, or the mannequin had to go everywhere we did.

The scenario was designed to produce failure and the instructors took the opportunity to ridicule our efforts. The point was to see how we reacted under stress and how we motivated and inspired our teams. And all the while the ever-present evaluation clipboard was just an arms' reach away.

Each candidate in my team got a turn to lead the others through one of these scenarios. When we finished, we had to run back to the starting point which was several miles away. We ran hard and finished with a respectable time and then got ready for the rest of the day's training events.

Not only was it winter and freezing outside, but the

physical training (or "PT") was intense. Our instructors PT'd us into the ground. We worked out for three to four hours a day, every day. We did calisthenics on the PT field, went on all-night conditioning hikes through the woods, climbed up steep hills with full backpacks weighing 50 pounds, and we broke through the ice and patrolled neck-deep in the bitter cold creeks and ponds. I've never been so wet, cold, or miserable in all my life. To this day, the cold weather still gets to me and reminds me of the winter spent in Officer Candidate School.

The level of physical exertion was grueling. Just when I couldn't go on any longer, it would be time to step off on a four-mile run through the woods or run the obstacle course several times. I would have to dig deep mentally to keep going. This went on day after day. The goal wasn't to see who was the fastest or strongest, but to see who had mental and physical courage and the commitment to not give up.

After the first four weeks had passed, candidates were given the opportunity to withdraw from the school or Drop on Request. The common slang for it was DOR.

Out of 256 candidates, we lost a quarter of our ranks at that point. Most of the candidates who left Officer Candidate School were academic types who liked the novelty of being a Marine Corps officer but couldn't reconcile themselves to the reality of what it entailed. Other candidates struggled to adjust to the intense pressure or lacked the drive to see it through. Some candidates couldn't endure the physical training. There is an adjustment to the military mindset, and some candidates simply were not Marine Corps material.

Whatever the personal reason, each candidate could choose whether to stay or leave from that point on. That is one of the major differences between enlisted basic training and Officer Candidate School. There is no quitting option in basic training. The Marine Corps basically owns you in basic training, and whether it takes you 13 weeks or 33 weeks to complete the training, you are staying until you finish, barring serious injury. The quickest way out of basic training is simply to gut it out and finish on time.

By contrast, during the training to become a Marine Corps officer, candidates had the choice to leave or could be forced out. The Marine Corps wants the best of the best to become officers, and my driving goal was to be one of them. I knew that I absolutely had to stay in and see it through. I could not go back to my enlisted reserve unit as a failure. I just couldn't. The only way I was leaving was if I was kicked out, or in a full-body cast or body bag.

The fourth weekend was a turning point in the program. Not only could the candidates drop, but we were now given a day and a half off from training every week. We were allowed to leave the base on Saturday and go wherever we wanted, as long as it was within 70 miles of the base. The only other rule was to be back in the barracks by 5 p.m. Sunday evening.

This was amazing! We were able to put our civilian clothes back on and get away from the base and the instructors and sort of recharge our batteries. The majority of candidates pooled their resources and rented hotel rooms and caught up on sleep. Some of the guys had family in the area and went home for the weekend. Others just stayed in the barracks and slept in their racks (beds). Some guys had the nerve to go out to the bars and clubs in the area to party. A couple times I thought briefly about joining them, but I knew the dehydration from drinking and lack of recovery time would only make Monday morning training that much harder. I had a couple of beers here and there during the time off, but left alcohol alone for the most part.

The fifth week started in hard and heavy. Now that the dead weight of the original candidate pool was gone, the instructors began to focus on teaching. We learned combat tactics, land navigation, military history, and drill manual exercises. More advanced physical training also came into play, such as conditioning hikes and combat assault obstacle courses. Even though the training had changed, the evaluations never stopped. We were constantly being screened on leadership, decision-making ability, and self-confidence levels.

If a candidate was not performing according to expectations, they were sent to a performance evaluation board where they had to make their case to remain in the program. Unless the candidates could convince the board as to why they should stay, they were sent home.

As the weeks progressed, more candidates dropped on request or were put on the five, seven, and nine-week performance evaluation boards. Most of the candidates that were sent to those boards were never seen again. I lived with constant fear that I would be called to appear before one of the boards, but it never happened.

Candidates were also dropped for medical reasons. The physical training regimen was so demanding that stress fractures, shin splints, and broken bones were very common. If an injury was too severe to continue training, the candidate was sent home. Some candidates were allowed to return to Officer Candidate School once they healed, but it was rare and they had to start from the beginning. More often than not, getting hurt and going home meant the end of the Marine Corps officer dream.

In my mind, I had nothing to fall back on and if I dropped out, I would not be able to face the people back home again, so I kept my head down and pressed on. I was fortunate enough to have enough strength and stamina to survive the physical training. I didn't quit, even when I developed a painful stress fracture in my right ankle six weeks into the course. I knew that if I chose to leave or was medically dropped I would most likely not receive another shot at becoming an officer.

This mindset of the Marine Corps is due to the fact that

there is always another candidate vying for an officer slot. The rigors of combat force Marines to endure extreme hardship. Weakness is not allowed. So instead of quitting, I went to the medical clinic every morning and had my right leg taped from knee to toe and I downed pain pills by the dozen. My leg never stopped hurting, but I only had four weeks until graduation. I resolved in my mind and heart that I could heal after I graduated, so I gutted it out.

During the ninth week of training, we went through our final evaluation exercise, Small Unit Leadership Exercise #2, or SULE 2. We started that Tuesday morning like any other, with breakfast and physical training, then classes, lunch, and so on. After dinner, we packed a forty-pound backpack and staged our gear for an all-night hike. At 10 p.m., we formed up outside on the parade deck and waited for the command to step off.

As only the Marine Corps could arrange, it began to rain. We waited and waited and then waited some more as the rain poured down around us. Around midnight the instructors showed up and we finally began the hike. We hiked on trails that took us through the forest, up and over steep hills, and down around lakes and across rivers. We hiked for hours through the night and finally came to the end of our trek at 6 a.m. the next morning. In six hours, we had hiked nearly fifteen miles. But the event was not over yet.

We were given a light meal and told to separate into our 13-man squads for the next portion of SULE 2. Just like SULE 1, this final event was leadership and scenario-based, only much more complicated and demanding. Each candidate would have an opportunity to lead his squad through a tactical scenario and would be graded on his planning, leadership, ability to inspire his men, and execution of the mission.

A Marine Corps squad is made up of thirteen Marines, so we had thirteen scenarios to get through, with each candidate leading one of the scenarios. Each scenario was also more than a mile away from the previous one and we had to run from mission to mission. The scenario evaluations were exhausting. We had been awake since 5 a.m. the previous morning with little food and nearly no rest, and we'd already hiked six hours all night long and covered fifteen miles. By grit and willpower, thirteen missions and fifteen additional miles later, we completed the exercise. As we crossed the finish line at 5 p.m., Wednesday afternoon, we all knew that we had passed the last test of Officer Candidate School. Graduation was finally in sight.

After ten weeks of brutal training, the candidates that were still standing were allowed to graduate. Of the original 256 candidates that began, only 173 remained; we had lost one in three. Our families arrived the day before graduation in March 2005, and we were allowed to spend several hours with them. Just like in basic training, I was able to give my family a short tour of the Officer Candidate School grounds. I showed them the PT fields, the obstacle courses, the classrooms, and the dining facility. Then we went over to the main part of Quantico to do some shopping. They dropped me back off at my barracks around 5 p.m., and I joined the other candidates in my platoon to get the squad bay cleaned and packed, our uniforms prepared, and our paperwork finalized.

On the morning of graduation, our families gathered in the stands along the Parade Deck. We marched out in platoon formation and went through a choreographed drill routine to demonstrate what we had learned to our families. After that, the commanding officer of Officer Candidate School gave a speech about the struggles, trials, and training that we had endured all winter. He told our families how proud he was of us and that it was an honor to induct us into the Marine Corps. Since I was already a Marine at this point, I must confess that the wonder and grandeur of the moment was somewhat less for me this time around. I had stood on the Parade Deck at Marine Corps Recruit Depot in San Diego for this ceremony less than two years before, so the second time around just wasn't the same. This time, I was looking ahead to the commissioning ceremony where I would become an officer.

As the speech ended, our instructors moved through our ranks and handed out the Eagle, Globe, and Anchor devices. Since I was a prior Marine, I already had mine, but it still felt good to receive a second one to mark the occasion. After the graduation ceremony, we turned our weapons into the armory and departed the OCS grounds. We were all Marines now, but not officers yet. We needed to change into a more formal uniform before we were actually commissioned and given the rank of Second Lieutenant.

At 2:00 p.m. that afternoon, all of us gathered in Little Hall on base and with our families looking on, the commissioning officer, a brigadier general, told us to stand and raise our right hands and swear the Oath of Office. After swearing the oath, we became commissioned United States Marine Corps officers. Then our families pinned our rank insignias to our uniforms and it became official.

That is the moment that I remember from graduation day. I had never been prouder in my life. As a new Marine officer, I had accomplished something that very few Americans do. I was struck by how far I had come and that I was part of something so much bigger than myself. It was a pivotal moment for me. I resolved to build on what I had accomplished and apply the same determination and self-discipline that had propelled me to become a Marine officer to the rest of my life.

7

After my graduation and commissioning, the Marine Corps gave me a brief ten days of leave, and then I was to report to The Basic School, also located in Quantico, Virginia. Since my family had driven to see me graduate, I rode back to Ohio with my mom and middle brother. We arrived the next day and I set about making plans to see family and various friends. I decided to spend a few days back in Grand Rapids, Michigan because I wanted to see my college friends that were still in the area, now that I was a Marine Corps officer. I had a great time visiting with everyone and the ten days were over too soon. When it was time to head back, I filled my car with the few possessions I owned and began the drive back to Quantico. The Basic School was waiting for me.

The Basic School is a six-month school for brand new Marine Corps Second Lieutenants. Every new Marine officer has to attend and graduate the school in order to advance to the next step of officer training. Failing could result in having one's commission revoked and being discharged from the Marine Corps. If Officer Candidate School could be compared to the job application and a hiring process, then

The Basic School was the introductory training period. There were multiple student training companies in The Basic School, each with about 250 new officers. My training company was Charlie Company and was further broken down into platoons; I was in the 6th platoon.

We began training on April 11, 2005. The first day was spent on basics, like getting our room assignments, heading to the armory to draw our M16 rifles, and going to supply and receiving all of our field gear. We would be spending a significant amount of time in the field, so our supply issue consisted of a large rucksack, a sleeping mat, gas mask, sleeping bag system with layers to protect against the elements and varying temperatures, and little odds and ends that would make living in the woods a little easier. The barracks were arranged in a Jack & Jill suite style configuration, essentially two bedrooms joined by a common bathroom. There were four Marines to each suite.

After we received our barracks room assignments, we spent several days forming into training platoons, completing our medical in-processing, and receiving all of the study guides and course work. Over the next six months, we would complete a total of 1,800 classroom hours. The introductory week ended with an initial Marine Corps physical fitness test. I was in excellent shape and did very well in each of the three events. I completed the maximum number of pull-ups and crunches, 20 and 100 respectively, and clocked a good time for the 3-mile run.

The following day we started our new routine. Classes began at 7 a.m., we broke for lunch at 11 a.m., resumed at noon, then wrapped up for the day around 5 p.m. After classes were over for the day, students were allowed to spend the rest of their evening at their own discretion. I always went to the gym on base and worked out after classes.

The classroom portion of the school continued for the entire six months, but the teaching was heavily concentrated during the first two months. The classes covered a wide array of topics, including military history, the psychology of warfare, battle tactics, land navigation, medical triage, military justice, logistics, and intelligence. The training also included practical application on weapon systems. We were timed on how fast we could disassemble and reassemble machine guns and mortar systems. We also spent time on the grenade range and the demolition range. The course work and practical training were rigorous, but I loved every minute. The training confirmed more and more in my heart that the career path of a Marine officer was the one for me.

After the first month of coursework and training, we spent two weeks at the rifle and pistol ranges practicing how to properly shoot our weapons. The standard weapon used by Marines is the M16A2 service rifle. As officers, we had to qualify with a side arm as well. An entire week was devoted to the fundamentals of building a good shooting position, breath control, and aiming. A second full week was devoted to nothing but practicing a set course of fire and then qualifying on the M16 and the pistol. The Marine Corps wants trained marksmen who can drop their targets from 500 meters away with one shot. In battle, when the confusion of war is thick and the bullets are flying, the training instilled in Marines keeps them collected and their shots accurate.

After three months of training, we began week-long field exercises. Each field exercise, or FEX, as it was called, was designed to teach basic fighting tactics and then build on them with real-life scenarios. We covered the making of platoon fighting positions from a defensive standpoint and then moved into the offense and attacked our brother platoons. We fought through gas attacks and did urban operations in mock towns. We also used simulation rounds (i.e. paint balls) during squad patrols on staged enemies.

The field exercises added a whole new level of realism to the classroom concept of combat. Learning tactics in the classroom provided the foundation for real combat, but nothing could beat live training. Marines have a saying, "We fight how we train." The more realistic the training, the better that Marines execute the task when doing it for real. At the time, the Iraq war had been raging for two years, so all the more, we knew that there was about a 100% chance that we would soon find ourselves there. It gave us an incredible incentive to soak up all that we could. The training would help keep us and our fellow Marines alive.

During these FEX events, we slept under the stars each night whether it rained or not; we never had tents or any sort of covering. Instead, we would huddle together in 13-man squads and then hunker down in our sleeping bags. If it rained, our waterproof sleeping bag shells did their best to keep us dry, but most of the time we ended up soaked. I remember more than one torrential downpour that would cause a river of water to run between my back and the sleeping bag. We ended these FEXs tired, filthy, and beat up, but we enjoyed them nonetheless because we felt like we were doing *real* Marine stuff with our brothers-in-arms.

AFTER JAM-PACKED DAYS OF COURSEWORK AND EXERCISES, WE were given "liberty" each weekend. Marine Corps liberty is the civilian equivalent of going home in the evenings or over the weekend. Officially, a Marine is always on duty, twenty-four hours a day, 365 days a year. Since the Marine Corps is the nation's emergency 9-1-1 force, liberty can be canceled at any time, but we looked forward to this standing privilege. During liberty, I could leave the base, visit friends or relatives, head up to Washington D.C., or simply hang around the barracks and relax. It was my own time to do as I saw fit. If I wanted to PT at the gym or catch up on sleep or be outside all weekend, I could do that. Or if I wanted to head up to

Washington D.C. and party, well I could do that too. As time
moved on during my time at The Basic School, I found the
desire to drink creeping back into my life.

The unwritten rule in the military is to work hard and play
hard. Because of the rigorous training regimen throughout the
week, I looked forward to relaxing on the weekends, gathering
with friends, and knocking back a few cold ones. Drinking just
came with the job. A popular spot on base was a bar in our
barracks called *The Hawk*. I had never heard of a bar being
located *inside* the barracks; the whole notion seemed
counterproductive to me, but this bar was open to any
student, any instructor, any permanent personnel stationed at
Quantico, and any other United States Marine who felt like
stopping by for a drink. When 5 p.m. on Friday rolled around,
or 1700 in military time, many of the young officers—and
myself—could be found at *The Hawk* for happy hour. We
drank some beers, then headed out for dinner and on to the
rest of our weekend.

As I started to mingle more with my Marine Corps peers
after hours, something bizarre started to happen. I began to
experience some of the same social confusion that I had gone
through during my early years at college. Once again, I was in
a large setting of people, joined together with a common,
driving goal. This time, instead of a collegiate education, the
purpose was Marine Corps training and development. And
just like before, I felt the pressure to fit in and be noticed for
something.

At any given point during the year, there were
approximately seven training companies at The Basic
School, and each company was coed. In some respects, The
Basic School was similar to a small college campus. People
banded together outside of training and social groups were
formed. Much like my high school and college years, I found
out that I didn't quite fit in with the mainstream social
scene. Many of the other second lieutenants were prior

enlisted Marines. While I had that going for me as well, some of the other prior enlisted had already been to Iraq or Afghanistan and actually fought in battle. Some of the young officers had been all-star sports figures at their universities, or some had advanced degrees in law or medicine. There were even Naval Aviators who had chosen to leave the Navy and join the Marine Corps to fly F-18 Hornet fighter jets. By comparison, I was just a C-grade college student who had somehow managed to make it through basic training and Officer Candidate School. I felt my confidence waning.

During undergrad, I used my willingness to buy alcohol for minors as a means to be part of the social crowd and make myself known. As a Marine officer at The Basic School, that didn't work for me. Everyone was over twenty-one, so no one needed me in that way. Even though I had achieved an upgraded status as a Marine Corps officer, that description applied to all of us at The Basic School. We were all Marine officers and equals in the technical sense, but I felt that I was still on the outskirts of the social scene because nothing really made me stand out from my peer group.

This renewed social discomfort stemmed also from my stutter. I was still self-conscious about it, even though I had learned to cope. I had also been an introvert for my entire life. While I enjoyed close friendships with select people, large group settings or the need to impress lots of people were not situations I sought after. Outside of my closer friendships, I could deal with people when life demanded it, but I was much more comfortable being alone with myself.

Being alone was safe because I wasn't vulnerable to ridicule because of my stutter, or to people's expectations of what the ideal Marine officer should be. So, while my fellow officers banded together and enjoyed every weekend together, I felt at odds and thus, I began to keep to myself more and more. I didn't realize it at the time, but as I gradually withdrew, I found even more reason to drink alcohol to fill the void.

In my new solo mindset, a typical weekend for me kicked off on Friday around 5 p.m. after training had ceased for the week. If I decided to hang around the barracks that weekend, I would go down to the dining hall for dinner. The dining hall offered a wide variety of food and many healthy options. Afterwards, I'd return to my room, pack a gym bag, and drive across the base to the gym. The commercial district of any Marine Corps base is called main side, and Quantico had a fantastic main side gym. I would stay at the gym for one to two hours, shower up, and then make my way back to The Basic School.

On the way back to the barracks, I always stopped at a 7-11 and purchased a twelve pack of beer and a pack of cigarettes, because they went together in my mind. If I really felt like drinking that night, I would pick up an additional six pack or a bottle of specialty beer to go along with my typical twelve pack. In those days, twelve beers were more than sufficient to get me drunk.

Throughout the evening, I surfed the internet, called friends and family, and watched movies on my laptop. Most of the students were long gone by this time, and I had the entire suite to myself. Even though I didn't realize it at the time, I was establishing a pattern of drinking alone. Before The Basic School, my drinking was always done with friends, roommates, or my brothers, and I equated drinking alcohol with being social and having a good time. At The Basic School, I wasn't drinking alcohol as a means of social interaction, but as a way of social withdrawal. Drinking became the way that I disconnected and recharged, and this new solo approach to drinking would plague me for years.

∾

EVEN THOUGH DRINKING ALONE WAS BECOMING MORE COMMON for me, I didn't always keep to myself during weekends at The Basic School. I bonded with a few of the other officers and I was particularly close with another fellow officer who graduated Officer Candidate School with me, a young Marine named Taylor. We would head out the two of us or we sometimes joined up with others to hit the bars together on a Friday or Saturday.

On those weekends, my routine started out the same. I went to the dining hall and ate dinner, sometimes alone, sometimes with others. Then I raced across to the main side gym, worked out, showered up, and then returned to my barracks room to get dressed for the evening. We would usually band together in groups of two to four. Any more than that and coordinating the activities became problematic; too many guys wanted to do too many different things.

Our group would typically end up either in Old Town Alexandria, or on M Street in Georgetown. Both districts boasted a vibrant party scene full of college kids, young professionals, civilians, and fellow servicemen. By the time we all arrived in one of those areas, it would be nearly 10 p.m. Starting at one end of the street, we worked the bars going in the opposite direction.

Old Town Alexandria is a historic neighborhood in Virginia on the banks of the Potomac River, with cobblestone streets, colonial architecture, and waterfront views of the nation's capitol. Old Town has several Irish pubs that are very popular with Marine officers, and we usually ended up closing down the night in one of them. I liked Old Town the best of our drinking destinations because it was historic and quaint, with a friendly vibe. The atmosphere encouraged relaxation, laughter, and good times, and I usually partied like it might be my last time.

If my friends and I didn't party in Old Town, then we often ended up in Georgetown on M Street. Georgetown is a well-known neighborhood in Washington D.C. full of high-end shops and boutiques, art galleries, restaurants, and bars along the waterfront of the Potomac. Famous homes and historic landmarks abound in Georgetown, and the neighborhood is the oldest and one of the most beautiful in the nation's capitol. The sidewalks were full of students from Georgetown University and young professionals such as doctors and lawyers. Certainly, M Street seemed like a different world than our Marine training world.

Pretty girls abounded in Georgetown, but the women on M Street also seemed to look down on me and my fellow officers. Not because of anything that we had done, but because we were Marines. Despite large numbers of military patrons frequenting the bars, I found that we were not always welcome or looked on in a favorable light. Marines have a certain haircut that is instantly recognizable. Some Marines would get very drunk and pick fights with other people and then get thrown out of the bars onto the street. This seemed to happen every so often in Georgetown. I found this to be problematic, and I didn't like being part of the spectacle. So if I had anything to say about it, we went elsewhere to party.

The final partying location, Adams Morgan, was my last choice. If M Street was another world from our Marine training environment, then Adams Morgan seemed to be an entirely different dimension. Adams Morgan is a stretch of eclectic bars, music venues, and multicultural restaurants spanning 18th Street in Northern Washington, D.C. The neighborhood is colorful and quirky, with a crowded nightlife scene. Students, hippies, philosophers, and professionals all come to party in Adams Morgan, and it's also easy to spot druggies on the corners and general low-lifes milling around. I didn't care for it much, and the dislike seemed to go both ways. For my part, I felt that some of the unsavory characters frequenting Adams Morgan were beneath me as a Marine Corps officer and I wanted to keep my distance.

I felt most at ease in Old Town Alexandria at the friendly pubs where they loved Marines. But even though I remember many good times while out with my buddies, I still had not learned anything about exercising self-control while drinking. In fact, I specifically remember one night of partying in Old Town that could have turned out badly for me. On this specific night, I headed to Old Town with three of my friends, and I was driving. The plan was to party hard, rent two hotel rooms and sleep it off, and return to Quantico the next day.

We started at one end of Old Town and headed up the street, stopping at bars along the way for a drink or two, and then moving on to the next one. Shortly after midnight, we ended the night at our favorite Irish pub, or so I thought. I got up to use the restroom, and when I came back, my friends were gone. I assumed that they must have moved outside or on to another bar and were so drunk that they had forgotten me.

I quickly paid my tab and went outside to see if they were having a smoke. They were not there. I staggered up and down the street looking for them, checked a few bars, but I didn't find them. By then, I was hurt and angry and very drunk. I wondered if they had forgotten about me after all or whether they had left deliberately.

Regardless of what had truly happened, I wasn't thinking clearly and I made a foolish decision. I decided to leave Old Town and drive back to Quantico alone and drunk. Even though I had driven everyone up to Old Town, I figured they could find their own way back to base. I wasn't going to stay in Old Town. First, I didn't know if my friends had booked a hotel already or not and I didn't want to purchase another room if they had already done so. Not only that, I wasn't even coherent enough to walk into a hotel and rent a room myself. My friends were not answering their cell phones, and I couldn't sleep on the street or in my car, so I decided to risk it like back in my college days.

I got into my car and onto the highway, set the cruise control, and made my way south on the 35-minute drive back to Quantico. I remember wondering whether I still had the driving skills from back in college when I used to drive drunk regularly, and it seemed that I did. Thankfully, I made it back to Quantico without being pulled over. Again, a DUI as a new Marine officer would have spelled the end of my career, but in my reckless, drunken state I had been willing to take the chance.

I pulled up to the back gate of The Basic School and parked my car in the drunk lot. This was a parking lot a little way down the hill and out of sight from the back gate where students could park their cars if they had been drinking and weren't sober enough to drive through the gate. The gate guards were young enlisted Marines and they were given additional time off if they could catch and bust a young officer coming through the gate drunk and operating a vehicle. They loved the challenge. It would be a feather in their cap to spell the end of the officer's career—over before it even got started. That was not going to be me.

I parked in the drunk lot and started walking the few hundred yards up the hill towards the back gate. As I approached the gate, the guards saw me and I got my identification card ready. I showed it to the guards and they saluted me, as was protocol for an enlisted person to an officer. Their eyes bored into me like lasers; they knew I was drunk, but because I wasn't driving, they couldn't do anything about it. They also realized that I *knew* that they couldn't do anything to me, and that knowledge only incensed them more. I leveled a sarcastic comment their way and walked on through the gate and up the hill to my barracks room. I still had a couple of beers in the fridge from the night before, so I changed out of my clubbing clothes, turned on the television, and cracked a cold one.

The next morning, I felt a little disgusted with myself.

Green and wet-behind-the-ears as I was, I was still a Marine Corps officer and I hadn't displayed officer-like behavior the night before. All I did was strengthen the reckless officer stereotype. I never should have put myself in a drunken situation without a plan to spend the night somewhere, I never should have gotten behind the wheel and driven drunk, and I shouldn't have taken advantage of the gate guards by treating them with sarcasm. They were only doing their jobs. I resolved in my heart to do better in the future.

As the summer and early fall of 2005 wore on, my time at The Basic School drew to a close. The last two months were spent taking academic and physical fitness tests and getting orders to my follow-on schools. My military occupational specialty, or MOS for short, had been selected a few weeks earlier around the halfway point of the cycle.

To choose the MOS, the leadership of my training company conducted a straw poll and each second lieutenant ranked all of the 22 MOS's in the order that he or she most desired. Once we submitted our wish list to the leadership, the instructors did their best to grant those wishes according to our aptitudes and the needs of the Marine Corps.

I felt that logistics was the best occupational fit for me because it seemed to blend with my economics education and my enlisted occupational specialty of supply chain management. Plus, I was thinking about life after the Marine Corps. Becoming a tank officer or special forces officer would have been incredible, but how many tanks does a person see patrolling down Main Street? I figured that logistics would be practical for me even outside of the Marine Corps. As it turned out, my instructors thought logistics would be a good fit for me also. Once I was formally assigned to the logistics occupational field, I received orders to logistics school and to Camp Lejeune, North Carolina. That would be my first duty station.

I continued to drink twelve packs on Friday and Saturday

nights, with bouts of partying in Old Town or D.C. with friends. To be honest, my now-habitual drinking didn't bother me. I acknowledged that my drinking had been out of control back in college, but now as a Marine and having achieved officer status, I felt that I could better handle myself. Alcohol was no longer necessary for cool status. It was simply a relaxation tool for me, and I felt that my drinking was well-deserved.

MY TIME AT THE BASIC SCHOOL CONCLUDED WITH TWO major events, both heavily steeped in tradition and drinking—the Field Trip and the Mess Night. The first event involved an actual field trip to Gettysburg, Pennsylvania. The Civil War battle of Gettysburg was a topic of study in our military history classes, and several weeks before graduation, my entire class loaded up on white buses and drove up to Gettysburg to tour the battlefield.

We left early in the morning and arrived by 9 a.m. Tour guides met us at the visitor center and led us on a play-by-play tour of the battlefield. It was an incredible time. At each stopping point, our instructors walked us through the tactics and mindsets of the generals and the soldiers that had fought more than 150 years ago. I had always loved history, but merging history with military strategy that day was especially interesting to me.

After touring the entire battlefield, we drove to the nearby home of a Marine Vietnam veteran for a barbecue. The owner had a long-standing affiliation with The Basic School and repeatedly offered his property for The Basic School field trips. The gentleman's home was a large property on the outskirts of Gettysburg with acres of developed land and a stately house modeled after a ranch style villa. The central part of the house was large and square with a separate wing adjoining the center. The landscaping was immaculate. Manicured walkways and shrubs decorated the front, while an enormous brick-laid patio covered part of the back yard. Several large brick fire pits and large brick grills and ovens were strategically placed in and around the patio as well. Surrounding the back edge of the patio were fir trees and more shrubbery.

Each of us had been instructed to pack a two-man tent, an overnight bag with a hygiene kit, and a change of clothing. The tents were pitched in neat rows along the south side of the property. Directly off the rear of the house was a large brick and flagstone patio where tables overflowed with kegs of beers, bottles of whiskey, barrels of potato salad and coleslaw, mountains of steaks, and seemingly countless boxes of cigars.

My entire training company of 250 students and instructors gathered around an elevated platform and our host took the stage. He welcomed us to his property and told us a little of his time in the Marines and of his deployments to Vietnam. He encouraged us to stay the course and to serve the Marine Corps with honor. We all raised our glasses and toasted our generous host, the Marines, and our brotherhood. Then our instructors made their speeches and their toasts. Each new speech required us to refill our glasses so that we could keep up. By the time the speeches and toasts were over with, we were well on our way to being drunk. Then the steaks were ready and we all began to eat. Music blared and we partied well into the evening.

Even though students and instructors have a natural barrier between them, as the alcohol flowed, that barrier came down and we treated each other as equals. The barrier would return the next day, but for that night, it was broken. I remember playing drinking games with my instructors and laughing like it was the most natural thing in the world. Finally, around 2 a.m., everyone was partied out and we crawled into our two-man tents and went to sleep. Some of the young officers just passed out and slept in the grass where they dropped.

We woke up the next morning feeling like death warmed over. On the drive home, the bus drivers likely received a contact high from all of the residual alcohol seeping out of our pores. We felt horrible but counted ourselves as fortunate for having enjoyed such an incredible time.

My training company set a new Basic School record with that field trip. The 300 of us drank thirty-two full kegs of beer, almost forty bottles of liquor and smoked more boxes of cigars than I can count. In fact, the party was so wild and crazy that The Basic School eliminated the Gettysburg Field Trip from the training schedule for follow-on classes. Our class had gotten too wild and out of control. The risk of law suits, Congressional investigations, and waning public opinion meant that there was just too much liability. I was glad to have experienced the last iteration of the event, however.

The final event of The Basic School was the Mess Night. A Mess Night is a time-honored and formal tradition in the Marine Corps. The name comes from the Marine Corps' naval roots. On ship, officers ate meals at the Officers' Mess; basically, a portion of the ship designated for that function. Over the years, a Mess Night has come to refer to unit events modeled after those early traditions. A Mess Night is conducted at the discretion of each battalion-level commanding officer. Mess Nights are held in training commands, supporting commands, and operational commands. Every attendee wears their most formal version of the dress blue uniform for Mess Night.

On the night of our Mess Night, I remember the banquet hall was decorated with colorful flags and banners, and the tables were arranged in long rows with ornate floral centerpieces. At the head of the banquet hall was a table where the President of the Mess, his guest of honor, and the official party were seated. Attendees took their seats and a formal color guard entered and posted the colors. Once the United States and Marine Corps flags were properly addressed and posted, the Adjutant began the formal proceedings.

Each Mess Night has a scripted portion that is part humorous and part serious. There are formal toasts, each with a different kind of alcohol involved. Then it is time for dinner and the script continues. On that night, a large side of roast beef was wheeled out on a cart and brought to the President of the Mess, in this case, the honor graduate of our class. As tradition dictated, he stood up in front of the meat, cut a small piece and tasted it. Then he raised his voice and addressed those in attendance, saying, "I declare this beef to be tasty and fit for human consumption," and then dinner was served.

During dinner, any Marine had the right to address the President of the Mess and ask for permission to speak. If permission was granted, the Marine would proceed with a formal charge against a fellow Marine, usually something ridiculous like accusing someone of bad training, wearing his uniform incorrectly, or an embarrassing moment. Punishments were a small fee or having to drink from a public alcohol bowl called the *Grog*. The entire proceeding would get more humorous as the night and the alcohol wore on.

The formal ceremonies adjourned around 10 p.m., and then we were free to continue the festivities on our own. There was so much beer, wine, and liquor left over from the formal party that we didn't have enough Marines to drink it all, but we sure tried. Gathered in various places in the banquet hall, outside in the Tea Garden area, in our rooms, in the hallways, and in the Green Carpet area, there was a complete breakdown of military bearing and self-control. Once again, the implied barrier between student and instructor vanished.

We all drank and caroused together, staggering in and around the buildings and making all kinds of noise. Around 2 a.m., I remember finally crawling up the stairs to my barracks room on all fours and heaving myself into my bunk. I passed out for a short time. At 3 a.m., one of our instructors barged into our room, woke us up, and dragged us back down to the party. He was so drunk that he was wearing half of his uniform and half of a student's uniform. The two halves didn't even match. He had on his dress blue bottoms and the green suit coat from the uniform of one of the students. Everyone drank so much alcohol that when we staggered out to formation the next morning, we were still drunk. And so were our instructors. Training was canceled for the day and it took the entire day for us to sober up. The crazy night of drinking and the requisite recovery period were both anticipated as part of the Mess Night experience.

In October of 2005, I graduated from The Basic School. My chosen occupational specialty was logistics, and I was to report to Camp Johnson in Jacksonville, NC for the three-month Logistics Officer's Course. I was familiar with the area because it had been the site of my logistics training a couple years prior as a junior enlisted Marine, fresh out of basic training. Now I would be going back to Camp Johnson as an officer. I was looking forward to experiencing the formal school environment in my chosen field now that I had some rank on my collar.

8

I arrived in Jacksonville, North Carolina for the start of Logistics Officer School in October, 2005. The city of Jacksonville is dominated by multiple Marine bases and installations, with Camp Lejeune being the main one. Nearby Camp Johnson is a smaller base in Jacksonville that houses the Marine Corps combat service support schools spanning the military specialities of logistics, maintenance, administration, and supply. I would be attending logistics school at Camp Johnson for the next four months.

Jacksonville is close to the ocean, and I found the beaches to be quite nice. Due to the miles of beaches on Camp Lejeune, the area is a significant location for amphibious assault training. Other than its beach location and the proximity to the Marine bases, Jacksonville offered little in terms of uniqueness, or arts and culture. Rather, it was a semi-economically depressed town with movie theaters, chain restaurants, and the typical selection of bars and night clubs. Novelty shops selling souvenirs, beach apparel, and military-themed trinkets were plentiful. Because Jacksonville catered to the whims and vices of the young Marines from base, the town also sported an abundance of liquor stores, pawn shops, strip clubs, tattoo parlors, cheap motels with *hourly* rates, and seedy dive bars. Simply put, Jacksonville seemed to exist for the sole purpose of giving Marines a place to live, let loose, and spend their money.

Since I was going to be stationed at nearby Camp Lejeune after I graduated logistics school, I was afforded the opportunity to live in town and not in the barracks. I moved into a house owned by another young Marine officer, a mile or two from the main gate of Camp Lejeune and about three miles from the front gate of Camp Johnson. I couldn't have asked for a more perfect location.

The house was situated in an upscale subdivision called Bryn Marr. The neighborhood was known for well-kept homes and manicured lawns. Our house was a large, two-story, single family home, and there were three other young officers living there besides myself. Because of the wars in Iraq and Afghanistan, the other officers were frequently gone on deployments, so I would have the place to myself for months at a time.

Logistics school began and I got right into a routine. Classes began at 7 a.m. and went straight through until 4 or 5 in the afternoon, Monday through Friday. We participated in organized physical training events every Monday and Wednesday morning, and our start time on those days was always at 5:30 a.m. Sometimes our class went for a long run through the woods, sometimes we ran the obstacle course, and sometimes we did Marine Corps Martial Arts. Physical training that early in the morning was never enjoyable, but our instructors let us go earlier in the afternoon to make up for the early start.

Logistics school was just shy of four months long and was broken up into phases. The first phase was the Maintenance and Acquisition Phase. During those four weeks, we covered many of the logistical concepts that we would be using to manage the maintenance of equipment, such as ordering repair components. We learned the Marine Corps processes and how the supply chain management system worked in order to buy and manage the things that our units would need to accomplish their missions.

The second phase was called the Amphibious Phase, due to the integration of the Marine Corps with naval ships and their movements across the globe. During this time, we studied amphibious operations, learned how to set up logistical supply depots on foreign beaches, practiced convoy and movement operations, and followed in trace of tactical units to provide logistical support. We learned how to calculate the amount of food, water, fuel, bullets, and medical supplies a tactical unit would consume per day, and we covered how to pre-stage gear and equipment in war zones so that the infantry would always have what they needed in order to successfully engage with the enemy.

The last phase of Logistics Officer School was the Embarkation Phase. This phase covered how to move people and equipment across the globe by land, air, and sea. We covered the processes for building load plans for airplanes and ships, and we learned how to move things over ground by railroad, commercial carriers, or with Marine Corps tactical trucking assets. Each phase was interesting in its own way, and I soaked up the knowledge as much as possible for future reference.

Logistics school ended with a week-long field exercise where we demonstrated everything we had learned. The field exercise (FEX) was conducted in some tactical training areas just south of Camp Johnson. Unlike the FEXs at The Basic School, none of the planning was done for us. As up-and-coming logistics officers, we were given the training objectives and then we had to plan our own FEX. We broke up into teams, with each team having a certain job.

One team was in charge of all the transportation to and

from the field. Another team had to source all of the gear, while another team locked on all the food and water required for a week. Another team had to come up with the convoy training specifics like routes, vehicles, drivers, and securing clearance for our movements through base Range Control. The last team was in charge of setting up our base camp in the field and establishing services like power, waste water, hygiene stations, bathroom facilities, and a mobile command station. We even received the benefit of several platoons of junior Marines that were on base in a holding pattern waiting for their own schools to start. This gave us a chance to command real Marines in the field as logistics officers.

The preparation for the final FEX began two thirds of the way through the school and ramped up during the last two or three weeks before execution. Everything was prepared and staged the Friday before we left for the field. We showed up Monday morning, drew our weapons from the Camp Johnson armory, and then climbed into our vehicles and began the 30-minute drive down to the training area. Setting up the base camp took the better part of that day. After everything had been set up, our mobile kitchen served dinner and we began to wind down for the evening.

The next day began a rotation of training events. Every officer had to rotate training stations during the week and serve in a number of billets. I served as a convoy commander on several missions, a command center watch officer, and a camp supervisor billet that we called "camp commandant." Each officer rotated stations during the week until everyone had a shot at each of the major billets. It was a long week, but a good one in terms of cementing all the knowledge we had learned.

Friday morning arrived and with it, the completion of the FEX. We began to tear down the camp, stow the gear, and get it packed up on the trucks. Once everything and everyone was loaded in vehicles, we moved back to Camp Johnson to unload and clean the gear before securing for the weekend.

The following week was graduation week. Monday started out bright and early as usual, and then we spent the rest of the week practicing for graduation, making travel arrangements, and closing out any administrative functions that were left to do. After graduation, we would be fully trained logistics officers ready for our first assignments in the Fleet. Most of the officers would be leaving for California or Okinawa as their first duty stations. Because I was going to be stationed at adjacent Camp Lejeune, my final week was pretty light. I was already living in my house and all of my arrangements were made.

Graduation day went smoothly, without much fanfare. After the grandeur of the graduation ceremonies for enlisted Marine Corps Basic Training, my college baccalaureate degree, Officer Candidate School, and The Basic School, the graduation from Logistics Officer School was rather small and simple. Families were not in attendance and there was no big ceremony. We gathered in the base chapel and our instructors made a few speeches, handed out an award to the class honor graduate, and then released us to begin our Marine Corps careers. The whole thing was over in less than 30 minutes. I was now officially a logistics officer in the U.S. Marine Corps.

My first assignment as a new officer was at Camp Lejeune, Second Maintenance Battalion. I wasn't thrilled about the assignment, but I resolved to do the best job that I could. I checked in on a Monday and after my second day, I was actually given new orders to go to Second Transportation Battalion to be a platoon commander in Support Company. I was ecstatic with this new development. Not only would I get to lead Marines in a command billet, but Transportation Battalion was responsible for tactical movements in Iraq and Afghanistan. There was a strong chance that I would get to deploy to the war zones and lead Marines in combat, which is something I wanted the opportunity to do. The idea of being one step closer to deploying was unnerving at first, but it also still seemed a long way off in the future, so I focused on leading my two newly assigned platoons as best I could.

After one month of serving in Support Company, I was called into the battalion commander's office and given new orders yet again. He told me that I had been picked to go to Third Battalion, Second Marine Regiment—or "3/2" for short—and would be deploying with the battalion to Iraq within six months. I was to transfer within the next few days to my new command to prepare for the deployment. Now that the assignment to deploy had arrived, I felt scared initially, but I soon got excited for the opportunity. This is why I had joined. The idea of deploying had always been in the back of my mind.

As a second lieutenant, my new assignment was among the best of the best in terms of career growth for a new officer. The Marine Corps orients everything around the infantry, and since 3/2 was an infantry battalion, I knew I would definitely see action. The assignment meant that I would get platoon command experience under my belt, plus I would do it all in a combat zone, and I would be serving within my chosen military occupational specialty (MOS) of logistics—the perfect trifecta. Looking back, I could not have carved out a better first assignment, aside from the danger of deploying. I was given my orders and transferred across the base to join up with my new command.

I took my place as a motor transportation platoon commander with 3/2 and was given the task of training a huge 75-man platoon in tactical convoy operations. Within a few short months, I would be leading them in battle halfway across the globe in Iraq. Was I nervous? Yes, but moreso, I wanted to excel at the challenge. I had joined the Marines during a time of war, and now that I was stepping in front of my new platoon for the first time, the war was in full swing. We were needed, and with that motivation, I led my platoon to the best of my ability as we prepared for the Iraq deployment.

Four months of training were ahead of us before we would depart the United States. Part of that training was a six-week training exercise at Marine Corps Base 29 Palms, located in the Mojave Desert in California. MCB 29 Palms is a desert base designed to give Marines an opportunity to train in the type of environment that is encountered in Iraq and Afghanistan. During our time there, we lived in the desert for six weeks and conducted numerous training missions. Marines have the mindset that we fight how we train, so we tried to come up with every possible combat scenario we could imagine and then train to that.

Each company in the battalion trained to their own mission. The infantry rifle companies trained on live fire ranges, conducted patrolling operations, and practiced clearing buildings in mock towns filled with scenario-based role players. The infantry companies interacted with the role players to simulate meetings with Iraqi village leaders and townspeople. The heavy weapons company practiced live fire ranges, mortar ranges, tactical vehicle patrols, and convoy operations. My platoon practiced tactical convoys and provided logistical support to the rifle and weapons companies that were operating out in the desert. It was great training for us and at the end of the six weeks, we felt that we were ready to take it to the next level and do it for real in Iraq.

During the six weeks of training in 29 Palms, we also simulated ground operating conditions in Iraq to get ourselves ready. We ate MREs, or "Meals-Ready-to-Eat," which are self-contained field rations that don't require heating or refrigeration. We went without showers for days at a time. At night we drove our vehicles into a large security circle, posted a watch, and set up our sleeping bags in the middle. When vehicles broke down due to the harsh environment, my maintenance teams performed a tactical movement to the downed vehicle, conducted tactical recovery operations, and brought the vehicle back to our main base camp to be fixed.

The Marines have a saying, "Never miss an opportunity to train," and we did our best to turn even the most mundane logistics task into an opportunity to train. The pressing goal was to execute our tasks well and put everything we had learned up to this point into practice, so that we could survive in Iraq. After six long and exhausting weeks of intensive deployment training, I left 29 Palms to return to Camp Lejeune.

SOMEHOW, BETWEEN CAMP LEJEUNE TRAINING EXERCISES AND my desert deployment training in 29 Palms, I still found time to drink and party. Several of my friends from The Basic School were stationed at Camp Lejeune as well, and we got together on the weekends to drink, relax, and spend time together. A typical weekend started late in the afternoon. My best friend lived several blocks away from me, so I'd drive over to his place and have a couple of pregame drinks, then we'd link up with others and all head out on the town.

Dinner was first. After assembling our group of friends, we called cabs and had them take us to our restaurant of choice. After dinner and several more drinks, we would decide where we wanted to go from there. There were many choices for partying in Jacksonville, but not a lot that I felt was worthy of my patronage as a Marine Corps officer. I had little personal interest in strip clubs or seedy dive bars, although I did go to both on several occasions. I found it more embarrassing than exciting to venture into strip clubs, but if I had enough alcohol in me, I could be convinced to do nearly anything I found uncomfortable. I typically went with the flow of whatever the group wanted to do.

On those evenings out, I bar hopped with my friends and usually ended up at one of the night clubs in town. I pounded drink after drink, smoked cigarettes, shot pool, danced a little, and flirted with the girls. Some of my friends would manage to hook up with some of the local girls and left the bar with them. I chose not to do that, partly because I held on to just enough of the morality that I was raised with, and partly because I felt I had too much to lose and I didn't want the drama.

The women in Jacksonville were well versed in the game. They would hit the clubs, wear revealing clothes, flirt heavily, get men to buy drinks for them, go home with them if needed, and then use them for their own purposes. On any given weekend, one could easily find local girls looking for free drinks and attention, or married women trying to hook up while their husbands were deployed. Prostitutes, identity thieves, and drug dealers also abounded amongst the women.

There was also the "professional wife." These professional wives married low-ranking, young Marines, and used them for the military benefits. More often than not, the girl would marry the Marine shortly before a deployment. While the new husband was overseas, the girl would spend the Marine's money and fully enjoy her life, date other men at will, and then file for divorce towards the end of her husband's deployment.

Upon his return, the divorce would be finalized and then she would set out to find herself another husband, making sure the next husband was of higher rank. She would come up with some story of spousal abuse to earn the pity of the new Marine sucker. Then the same series of events would happen all over again. Some of the professional wives had three or four divorces under their belts.

I personally knew several Marines who were victims of this type of situation. Granted, the young Marines were often looking for easy scores with the local girls, so much of the blame can be handed to the men as well. But due to the transient nature of the Marine Corps, one to three years was all a Marine spent in one area, and that didn't count deployed time. That set of circumstances made for an environment ripe with sinful living and people looking to take advantage. I saw the debacle unfold between one of my young Marines and a professional wife firsthand.

Several months before our Iraq deployment, one of my young Marines met a newly divorced woman in her 40's at a local bar in the next town over. He claimed he was in love with her after a month of dating and wanted to marry her. When my senior enlisted Marines and I found out about it, we counseled him not to go through with it. We would be deploying soon and the risk was just too great, and we had a suspicion of her true intentions. But several weeks before we flew out, they married anyway. All during the deployment, the woman sent care packages and love letters to my Marine. Seven months went by like this, but once we began the week-long process of leaving Iraq for the United States, she cut off all communication, cleaned out his bank account, and filed for divorce.

I remember coming home from the deployment and pulling up in our buses to the receiving area of Camp Johnson. A large tent and celebration had been set up to welcome us home. The wife met my Marine as he stepped off the bus and handed him the divorce papers. I had never seen a young man so crushed.

While I was never the victim of a professional wife, I made some poor decisions and ended up paying the price. Several friends and I were out one Friday night at a club in the oldest part of town. Of all the clubs in Jacksonville, this particular one happened to have the worst reputation. It was common knowledge on the street that a person could buy drugs or sex at this establishment. While I wasn't there for that purpose, I was still ready to get drunk.

As my friends and I drank, we started talking to several girls at the bar. After some time, someone suggested that we take the party back to one of our houses. Being drunk, I thought this was a great idea and offered my place up. We called for some cabs and headed to my house. Once we arrived, we all converged in the living room to continue drinking and listen to music.

While we were occupied with partying, one of the girls slipped into my home office and stole my laptop and a paper copy of my credit report that happened to be lying on my desk. After she'd stashed the stuff in her bag, she returned to the party and gave the signal to the other girls. They came up with an excuse about having to leave and they raced out of the house. What really happened was that we'd been duped and targeted by thieves.

Once I was clear-headed the next morning, I realized what had happened and called the police, but at that point, they could do little for me. They were quite familiar with this sort of crime and had little sympathy. I gave them the serial number of the laptop and they promised to scan the pawn shops for any activity, but they warned me that tracing the laptop would be next to impossible. True enough, I never saw that laptop again.

You would think that I would have cleaned up my act after getting robbed, but I didn't. I still wanted to drink and party and have fun; I only wanted to do it smarter. No more inviting groups of people back to my place if I didn't know them.

The spring ended and summer was soon upon me. That meant that my Iraq deployment was just around the corner.

~

In June 2006, I boarded a plane with the advance party and flew to Iraq by way of Kuwait. The advance party, or ADVON, as we called it, was a team of officers and senior enlisted Marines that deployed ahead of the main body and coordinated the arrival of the rest of the force. It was our job to link up with the unit that we would be replacing and coordinate living arrangements and equipment turnover, receive security briefings, and conduct tactical patrols to scout out the area of operations where we would be fighting. The rest of the battalion followed us several weeks later.

The ADVON gathered at Marine Corps Air Base Cherry Point, just 30 miles from Camp Lejeune, and prepared to fly out. Our regimental commander met us at the terminal and talked to us briefly. He encouraged us to go forth and do our duty and return victorious. Then he quoted a familiar verse of Scripture to spur us on, with a humorous, albeit blasphemous, twist. He quoted from the 23rd Psalm, *"Yea, though I walk through the valley of the shadow of death, I will fear no evil, for I am the baddest mother*** in the valley."* And with that motivating sentiment in our minds, we got on the plane and flew halfway around the globe to war-torn Iraq.

After the arduous trip, it felt surreal upon arrival to be in-country after all our training and preparation. We arrived at a base along the Euphrates River called Habaniyah, which was halfway between Fallujah and Ramadi. The base was a former British army compound that had been used during the late 19th and early 20th centuries during the height of the colonial days. Many of the original buildings were still there but in tremendous need of repair. We were going to occupy the base and use it as our center point for launching tactical operations in the area.

That particular area of Iraq, coined "the Shark's Fin", was lacking U.S. presence before our arrival, so we had a lot of work ahead of us. Since my military specialty was logistics, the primary mission of my platoon was to conduct tactical vehicle patrols along the main supply routes, or MSRs, and resupply convoys to all of our forward infantry positions. Because our battalion was spread out along the Euphrates River, we were on the road every single day. The frequency of our missions exposed us to numerous improvised explosive devices and enemy attacks on the roadways.

On one occasion, I was commanding a night time resupply convoy that was headed into the western edge of our territory to resupply several of our battalion's positions. The convoy included about seven vehicles carrying a resupply of fuel, water, food, and ammunition. Traveling under cover of darkness, we passed westward through a small town named Sadiqiyah and stopped at what was called the 611 Bridge. This was an overpass along Rt. 611 that bridged the north and south banks of the Euphrates River, and one of our infantry positions was located on top of the bridge on the southern riverbank. We parked our vehicles and hurried to offload our supplies so we could be on our way back to base.

As soon as we cleared the 611 Bridge, an Iraqi insurgent fired a rocket-propelled grenade from a minaret at a nearby mosque and hit one of our trucks containing the fuel tanks. The truck was engulfed in flames in an instant. Fortunately, the two Marines in the cab and the Marine in the machine gun turret were able to escape before the entire truck exploded. It all happened so fast that no one could tell what had happened.

Our adrenaline went into overdrive and those of us on the ground prepared to be attacked by an enemy force. Thankfully, the attack never came. We were able to cordon off the area with the burning truck and search for any further enemy threat. After gaining control of the situation, we called for a casualty evacuation and got the three Marines removed from the field. Thankfully, they only sustained minor injuries.

When it was deemed that all was quiet and safe, we returned to base to regroup.

On another occasion, I was leading a convoy back to our base after conducting resupply operations all day long. Our convoy approached a small town that was still several miles from base. It was late afternoon and the local markets should have been bustling with activity since the extreme heat of midday had passed, but everything was strangely quiet. Right away, we knew something was wrong. I was in the lead vehicle and I began to scan the road and the shoulder for anything that looked unusual. A favorite enemy tactic was to put improvised explosive devices in potholes or disguise them as trash and wait for an opportunity to strike.

We were nearly halfway through the market place before I saw it. Not more than five feet in front of our vehicle sat a shiny black box in a pothole. I saw the bomb too late. We rolled over top of the box and the bomb exploded. The sound was deafening. Smoke, dirt, and small debris ripped through the cab of our vehicle. We sat there for a moment, totally stunned and disoriented. Time seemed to stop for me. Little by little, I came-to and began to check myself and my three Marines for any vital injuries.

Miraculously, there were no penetrating injuries, just concussions from the impact. We were fortunate because the bomb had explosive force but no damaging shrapnel. The bomb had blown out the tires on our vehicle and damaged the frame, but other than that, we were alright. The radios in my vehicle were destroyed, but I was able to call out our status to the other vehicles using our personal walkie-talkies, and they relayed our status to our battalion command. We regrouped and our convoy was able to limp back to base where we were greeted with a hero's welcome.

The battalion staff had listened to our convoy's reports over the radio and wanted to be out at the entry gate to welcome us home. As we came through the gate and passed the battalion command building, Marines were lined up cheering and clapping their hands. The feeling was incredible. To have survived an enemy bomb and come back to the cheers of your fellow Marines! We waived our acknowledgement and continued to the motor pool to turn in our vehicles and then went on to medical to get checked out. I was humbled by the entire experience, but also proud at the same time. I had literally been *blown up* and lived to tell about it. I felt invincible.

I spent a total of seven months in Iraq on that first deployment. During that time, my platoon logged 235 combat missions and I personally commanded 115 of them. I was grateful to have outstanding Marines. They were fearless and professional in everything that they did. Our logistics missions enabled our infantry Marines to take the fight to the enemy on their home turf. My platoon carried out resupply missions, conducted tactical patrols, and oversaw troop and prisoner transport. We cleared fields with the potential for hidden explosives by burning out overgrown vegetation. We also destroyed key strongholds and blew up enemy installations.

Most importantly, throughout all these missions, I didn't lose any Marines under my command. Our battalion had nearly 1,100 Marines and sadly, 14 Marines from other platoons were killed in action. I had the misfortune of seeing some of them actually die in battle; all of them much too young.

I vividly remember seeing one young Marine drop after being shot by a sniper. He was hit in the neck and immediately crumpled to the ground, and he was gone shortly after that. I had a convoy nearby and we received the call to collect the body and take him back to base. As we loaded the fallen Marine into our vehicle, I remember seeing him drenched in blood from the neck down. It's not something you can easily forget.

In addition to deaths, more than 100 Marines were

wounded to one degree or another in other platoons. Somehow, my platoon scraped by with little to no injuries. Some people said that my platoon was incredibly lucky, but I believe it was more than that. I'm convinced that God protected us. Other than a few concussions here and there, all 75 of my Marines made it home in one piece.

9

I arrived home from Iraq in February, 2007. My unit was given nearly a month of leave and I used that time to travel to Ohio to see my family. When I wasn't on the road traveling or visiting family, I was drinking and partying with friends during my month off. I had lots of war stories to tell.

Soon after returning from my first deployment, I found out that I would actually be deploying again in the near future, this time to Afghanistan. I was stoked about the news. After reporting back to Camp Lejeune, I transferred out of my infantry battalion and joined an expeditionary unit that was scheduled to deploy in the early months of 2008.

The operational tempo of my new training package was so intense with field exercises and sea time that I didn't have time for drinking like I wanted, meaning that I couldn't drink every weekend. So, when I was able to drink, I did it at home. My reasoning was two-fold: I was drinking to relax after working hard and I was succumbing to the lesser of two evils. Drinking at bars and clubs with rowdy Marines or women on the prowl carried too many risks. It was safer to do my boozing at home. I could stock up on beer, snacks, and food, then just sit back on my couch and watch TV and drink. It was very peaceful. However, I can look back now and realize that I was also self-medicating.

One of the reasons that I began drinking so heavily and doing it alone was because I still felt like I was on the losing end with women. While there were girls a-plenty trying to hook up and the easy score was readily available, I had always struggled with Christian girls looking for meaningful relationships. In fact, something that happened shortly after my arrival in Jacksonville the previous year affected me greatly.

Shortly after starting Logistics Officer's School the year before, I promptly joined a local church that one of my roommates attended. Since I was going to church on Sundays, it curbed my habit to party on Saturday nights. Several weeks in, I met a girl at the church and asked her out. After two or three dates together, my training sent me to the field for my final exercise for logistics school.

Even though I was gone for only a week and we had parted well, she simply stopped talking to me once I returned. I didn't know why, and I never received an explanation. Just poof. She vanished from my life. The church was quite small and everyone knew everyone else's business, so it felt awkward. I simply stopped attending the church. Soon, I got busy with the six-month training cycle for my upcoming Iraq deployment and then I was overseas for seven months.

After I returned from Iraq, my roommate invited me to attend the same church with him again. I went one Sunday morning and saw the same girl that had cut me off a little over one year before. She was married and very pregnant. Seeing her with a husband and a baby already on the way hurt me deep inside.

Really? She had moved on that quickly? What was so wrong with me? Why was I so easy to cast aside? I knew she didn't discard me from her life because of a drinking problem.

She hadn't been exposed to that side of me. We'd only ever seen each other at church or during church activities. Things seemed to be going well, so why? I pondered the questions over and over in my mind and tried to figure it all out, but I never received clarity to my internal debate.

That experience unfortunately drove me to write church out of my life for the next year or so. Instead, I decided to throw myself into my job and the Marine Corps and doing whatever I wanted on the weekends. I could have looked for another church if I'd been truly serious about my walk with the Lord. But I wasn't, and so I didn't try to find another church to plug into. Instead, I took back my Saturday nights for the purpose of partying and chasing the wrong sort of girls, and I skipped church on Sundays.

Even though I subconsciously chose to sabotage my church life, I knew deep down that it was the wrong choice, just like I knew that all of the drinking and partying in college had been poor decisions. But I still wasn't ready to do business with God on His terms, so I chose to live my life the way that I wanted. That meant a lot of drinking at home, partying with friends when military training exercises allowed, and flippant dating with no intention for anything lasting. More and more, my life revolved around the meaning and purpose gained through the Marine Corps.

~

MY AFGHANISTAN DEPLOYMENT WAS QUICKLY APPROACHING. Throughout the spring, summer, and fall of 2007, my new battalion conducted training exercises to prepare us for the time we would spend in Afghanistan. I was now assigned to the Combat Logistics Battalion 24, attached to the 24th Marine Expeditionary Unit, or 24th MEU.

The Marine Corps is generally organized and deployed within the construct of a Marine Air Ground Task Force

(MAGTF). A MAGTF brings all the capabilities of a rapid, self-sustaining, tactical force together under one commander and can be deployed anywhere in the world in just a matter of days. The ability to deploy quickly and be self-sustaining is one of the reasons why the Marine Corps is typically the first military force to strike in a time of need. The Marines provide the fighting support until another military force arrives to provide the more sustained battle objectives.

The MAGTF has four elements: Command Element, Ground Combat Element, Logistics Combat Element, and an Air Combat Element. A MEU is the smallest form of a MAGTF and is usually deployed for six months on board an Expeditionary Strike Group, or ESG, comprised of several U.S. Navy ships with the mission of conducting combat operations within their international area of operation.

In my case, our MEU was tasked to go to Kandahar, Afghanistan and begin combat operations on land rather than the usual six-month sea-based deployment. My title was the "S-4" which meant that I was the principle logistics officer for my battalion. Much of my time was spent coordinating our capabilities, training our Marines on tactical convoy procedures, putting together logistical supply plans, and preparing and giving briefs to senior officers. We also did ship-to-shore training events where we practiced storming a beach from a naval ship. I loved nearly every aspect of the preparation activities.

Several weeks before we boarded planes to fly to Afghanistan, we embarked our equipment on commercial shipping vessels going across the Atlantic. The idea was to give the equipment a healthy head start before the personnel started arriving. Being a logistician, I was responsible for coordinating the embarkation of my battalion's gear in conjunction with the plans set by the S-4 for the MEU Command Element. If we timed it right, both the personnel and the gear would arrive in Kandahar around the same time.

The day to deploy finally arrived on March 8, 2008. We left Camp Lejeune on buses and headed to Marine Corps Air Base Cherry Point to meet up with the commercial aircraft that would take us across the Atlantic and into Afghanistan. Several refueling points were built into the flight path. We stopped in Bangor, Maine, then Frankfurt, Germany, and finally deplaned in the nation of Kyrgyzstan on a NATO coalition base named Manas.

We spent a week in Manas. Most of the time was spent getting organized and working through some initial orientation briefs; however, it struck me as unnecessary and boring to be there for an entire week. I was excited about getting to Afghanistan and taking the fight to the enemy, and being in Manas seemed to be a waste of time. The living conditions were transient and I couldn't wait to get out of there.

Finally, it was time to leave for Kandahar. We landed and spent several days getting set up on the ground. So much needed to be done. Unlike Iraq, where we basically arrived on a fully operating base, this time we had to build our operations from scratch. Even though Kandahar was a fully operating base also, we were staying in a remote corner of the base, far from the matured areas. We were going to be more or less on our own. We would be conducting our missions using mobile command centers that we had brought with us. Instead of sleeping in buildings, we would be staying in "hooches," which were large, multi-person tents set up over large wooden platforms.

Our communications Marines got right to work in setting up our computer terminals, internet connections, servers, and networks. I spent a fair amount of time getting our weapons armory, field ammunition supply point, motor pools, maintenance facilities, and camp services set up. All of it took coordination with our counterparts at MEU headquarters and various U.S. and NATO coalition forces on the Kandahar base.

The Kandahar base was the size of a small city with an estimated 19,000 people living and working on base. Some of the people were United States contractors providing logistics and infrastructure support. Others were European nations supporting the war effort. Still others represented U.S. agencies like the CIA, FBI, State Department, and the Defense Department. The base had paved roads with stop signs, traffic cops, a sewage facility, three large dining facilities, several gymnasiums, thousands of barracks-style living quarters, hundreds of work spaces, a full tactical airport, a fuel farm with hundreds of thousands of gallons in capacity, and local shops and vendors by the hundreds.

Located in the center of the base was an area called The Boardwalk which was a large, wooden boardwalk that formed a gigantic ring. Inside the ring were volleyball courts, a roller hockey rink, and a musical stage. Various shops and restaurants were located on the boardwalk. You could get a burger at TGI Fridays, grab coffee at Tim Hortons, or buy Afghan clothing and trinkets from local merchants. Professional musicians would come to the Kandahar base to support the troops and hold large concerts on the stage. The base was certainly impressive.

It took just under one month to receive all of our equipment, get fully set up and organized, and begin combat operations. In contrast to my Iraq deployment where our battle-space was rather small, with only a 30-mile section of the Euphrates River to patrol and defend, in Afghanistan we monitored all of Kandahar and Helmand Provinces, nearly 200,000 square kilometers. The ground combat element of our MEU, 1st Battalion, 6th Marine Regiment (called 1/6), pushed to the southwest to begin operating in the Marjah district of Helmand Province.

One of Afghanistan's primary sources of income is the

poppy plant, from which the drug heroin is made. Helmand Province was a key piece of real estate because of the numerous rivers and water basins in what was otherwise desert terrain. The abundant water supply allowed fields of poppies to grow by the thousands and the Taliban had laid claim to most of the fields and used the proceeds to finance terrorism.

One of our MEU's most important missions was to disrupt the poppy plant trade and cripple the Taliban's main source of income. The goal was to move in quickly, defeat any Taliban insurgents, help facilitate a working government, and then move on to the next hot spot. However, the Taliban decided to guard their source of income at all costs and the Marines encountered so much resistance in Marjah that the decision was made to stay put and continue fighting.

Our snipers and infantry Marines took it hard to the insurgents. Every day we heard reports over the radio networks of 10-50 Taliban killed. Miraculously, our own losses were minimal. The 1/6 ground combat element of our MEU fought hard every day, and the role of my combat logistics battalion was to support and resupply them to enable that fight to continue.

Providing logistical support to that many men and women in combat was challenging. We established trucking routes to contract the delivery of fuel to forward areas. We established aerial resupply routes, and our C-130 cargo planes were constantly in the air, moving troops and supplies back and forth across the provinces. We established supply depots at various forward operating bases so that Marines could come back from the fight, refit and rearm, get some rest, then head back out.

Once I'd worked to establish all of our resupply networks, my task was to manage and maintain the flow of goods and services throughout the region. Even though I was based in Kandahar, I flew across the provinces on a weekly basis checking up on my Marines and stopping in to talk with senior officers to see where the holes were and what we could do to fix them. It was exciting work.

Monday mornings often started with me giving a briefing to my battalion commander, visiting some logistical sites around the base, and then heading down a day or so later to the base flight line to catch a flight to another base. Sometimes I had to wait in the flight line terminal for eight hours or more in order to catch an open seat on a cargo transport to one of the bases. There were a couple bases I checked in on regularly as part of my logistical duties.

One of the bases I visited was a British army base called Bastian located in the west. Bastian had several fresh water wells and a bottling plant that provided purified, cold drinking water to that part of the country. Or I would fly to Forward Operating Base Dwyer to check in on our infantry Marines and make sure they had the necessary supplies and maintenance repair parts needed to keep their tactical vehicles on the road. After visiting the base for a day or so, it would be back to the flight line to catch a helicopter ride to a larger airport and then I would board a cargo transport back to Kandahar. Other times, I grabbed a helicopter ride and my week would end by flying route reconnaissance missions because we were always in the business of getting our eyes on new logistical supply routes.

Fortunately for us, the logistical networks and supply routes we established worked like a charm. Supplies and services moved so fluidly that our work was used as a model by Headquarters Marine Corps in the planning of future combat operations. The entire MEU was so successful that everyone received special medals of commendation for our performance. Personally, I greatly enhanced my skills at logistics and really began to hit my professional stride.

~

MY AFGHANISTAN DEPLOYMENT HELPED MY CAREER ON MANY levels. To be sure, I was still in the early stages of my Marine logistics career, but I was developing at a rapid pace. During the deployment, I was selected for the rank of Captain and was "frocked" less than three months later. Typically, when a Marine is selected for a higher rank, it can take over a year to actually pin on the rank, a wait time based on seniority. For a Marine that has been selected for a higher rank, frocking means that you get to promote early and are allowed to wear the insignia of the higher rank. While you do not receive the higher pay until a future point in time, being frocked gives the Marine the privilege of wearing the higher rank much sooner and the authority that comes with it.

While in Kandahar, the typical wait time from selection to promotion for the rank of First Lieutenant to Captain was fourteen months. I pinned on my Captain's bars in less than three months. I was being given the most difficult tasks and finding myself with access to higher levels of the Marine Corps and spheres of influence. I was excited about my future.

Combat operations ceased for us towards the end of September. The forward elements of our battalion began the process of retrograding their personnel and equipment back to Kandahar to be cleaned up and refitted. All of October was consumed with preparations for the return to the United States. An advance party returned home first. The advance party had the mission of getting back to Camp Lejeune and setting up our new work spaces and living quarters. Several weeks later the main body would follow, then the rear party. I flew back with our rear party. All said and done, our MEU had spent eight long months fighting in Afghanistan, and along with the rest of my Marines, I was ready to come home.

My flight home took me to Manas for another week of out-processing and re-orientation briefs. I used the time to catch up on exercise and sleep. We left Manas and flew to

Budapest, Hungary, then to Reykjavik, Iceland, and finally to Cherry Point in North Carolina, about 30 miles from Jacksonville. We touched down in the U.S. in the early evening and boarded buses to Camp Lejeune. My brother was a young Marine Corps officer at The Basic School at the time and he drove down from Virginia to welcome me back. He picked me up on base and we drove back to the house I was still renting in Jacksonville.

Finally back at home, I had a few beers to cut loose after the months of deployment. Marines are not allowed to drink alcohol while on deployment. Mixing alcohol and combat is a recipe for disaster, so drinking is banned. Some Marines are able to sneak alcohol into combat zones by having family members send liquor in mouthwash bottles or other containers, but the consequences are extremely severe if they get caught.

Having been deprived of alcohol for so long, some Marines can't wait to get home and get drunk on the first night. I know I felt like it. But I decided to stay sober that first night home because we had a formation the next morning before officially being placed on leave. The heavy drinking could wait a day or two, and besides, the holidays were just around the corner and that would provide plenty of time for drinking.

∼

NOVEMBER AND DECEMBER ARE GREAT TIMES OF CELEBRATION for the Marines. The Marine Corps birthday is on November 10 and the annual Birthday Ball is held on the adjacent weekend. Then a slew of festivity follows with Thanksgiving, Christmas, and New Year's Eve in quick succession, each one providing leave time.

For the Marine Corps Birthday and each federal holiday of the year, the Marine Corps is given a "96," or a ninety-six-hour liberty period. Essentially, it is considered to be a four-day weekend. These 96s would start on Friday morning with a battalion formation around 10:30 or 11 a.m. Our commanding officer would take some time to speak to the battalion about future events and reward certain Marines for jobs well done. We listened to mandatory safety briefs where we were told not to drink and drive, stay out of jail, etc. Then the commanding officer would secure us for liberty, and we would then be free to do whatever we wanted until we had to report for duty the following Wednesday morning.

These 96s were wonderful and we had ten of them a year, nearly one for every month. Sometimes I traveled home to Ohio for these short holidays and sometimes I stayed local. If I stayed local, I made plans with my fellow officers, or my brothers or a college friend would drive down and we would spend the four days drinking and grilling out.

By this point in my life, I was well over the bar scene. After returning from Iraq and especially after my Afghanistan deployment, I found that I desired my alone time on the weekends. I gave so much of myself during the week, let alone the energy expended during my two deployments, that I craved the entire weekend to be alone to recharge. I had dabbled in solo drinking during The Basic School and later after finishing logistics school, but this was the point in my life when drinking alone became the standard for me. Since alcohol was my favorite weekend pastime and since I craved alone time at my own house most weekends, the two activities went hand-in-hand, like peanut butter and jelly.

Each 96 provided an extended opportunity for me to drink heavily. After being secured from duty on Friday morning, I began my 96 routine. I started by leaving formation and heading straight to the gym. I lifted heavy weights for nearly two hours and then went for a five-mile run around the base. I ended up back at the gym and after showering, would head towards main side where the grocery and liquor stores were located.

I browsed the aisles of the grocery store and picked up steaks, chicken, bratwurst, and side dishes. Then I went next door to the liquor store and looked for a bottle of scotch or vodka, some mixers, and several cases of beer. After packing everything into my car, I would leave the base and head back to my house. As soon as I pulled into the driveway and got my supplies inside, I'd either mix a drink or crack a beer and set about planning what I wanted to do for the next four days. Naturally, anything I decided to do would need to be local because I would be too inebriated to drive anywhere. I wasn't opposed to seeing people, but if they wanted to get together, they would have to come to my house because I wasn't going to leave my place for anything.

During the first day, I did any yard work that needed to be done and I would clean my house from top to bottom, all of the time with a drink in my hand. I made sure to make any phone calls to family members before nightfall. Any later than that and my voice would be too slurred to be understood. I certainly didn't want my family getting on my case for my drinking habits. At that point, my parents weren't fully aware of the extent of my drinking, and I wanted to keep it that way.

As the evening wore on, I would watch TV and movies and play around on my computer. As soon as one drink was consumed, I'd pour another. On most 96's, I was passed out drunk by 1:00 a.m. At some point, usually the darkest hour of the night, I would wake up on the floor or couch or wherever I happened to drop. Then I would drag myself upstairs to my bedroom, crawl into bed, and pass out all over again. After waking up hours later, it would be time to make myself some breakfast and try to shake off the hangover. If I wasn't too hung-over, I went running for several miles and cleaned up a little before starting in with a repeat of the previous night's activities.

By the third day of the 96, I would have so much residual alcohol built up in my system that my body couldn't hold any more. Rather than chastising myself, I would be annoyed that I still had one full day of leave before having to report back to base, but couldn't drink because my body couldn't hold any more alcohol. It was like being cheated out of a day of fun.

At times, my weekend drinking caused me embarrassment. I remember drinking very late one Saturday night and passing out on the floor of my library which was adjacent to the central foyer of the house. I don't remember what I was drinking that night, but my pattern would suggest that I'd consumed eighteen beers or more. I remember listening to music on my computer one moment and the next I was waking up on the floor with sunlight streaming in the windows. I was laying half in my library and half in the foyer, and my roommate had just come down the stairs so that he could leave for church. He nearly tripped over me. He just looked at me like I was some sort of interesting beetle and asked me if I was alright. I mumbled something that resembled a yes, and then he actually stepped over me and walked out the front door.

Another time I had my laptop with me on the front porch as I drank the night away. I'd been chatting with people online and ended up falling asleep on the porch. I woke up the next morning stiff and soaking wet from the dew. Fortunately, my laptop was not ruined, but I shudder to think of what all of the passersby on the street thought when they drove past the house and saw me passed out on the porch.

I also had close calls with my parents. Each of them came to visit me at several points during my time in Jacksonville. After staying the night at a hotel, they'd come to my house on Saturday or Sunday to spend the day with me. They were eager to get the day started, but I was usually hung-over to the point where I needed an hour or two to get myself together. Even though my parents didn't drink themselves, I think they recognized the signs of a hangover—diminished awareness, bloodshot eyes, scratchy voice, and of course, the smell. When a person consumes as much alcohol as I did, there is always a tell-tale smell as the booze oxidizes out of the body.

I was careful to hide the evidence of my drinking as much as possible, and of course, I would lie to cover myself. It is humorous how people think they can fool their parents. I would *never* believe some of the tall tales that I told my parents to conceal the truth. But even though they suspected, I still don't think they realized to what extent I was drinking my weekends away.

By the early spring of 2009, I was ready to at least entertain the notion that I had a serious drinking problem. I was 29 years old, and my weekends revolved around drinking. Adverse effects were cropping up in my social life. I was keeping to myself more and more, and instead of pursuing healthy relationships with Christian girls, I was settling for online chats and meaningless flings.

I can recall brief relationships with a couple Christian girls that would come to a breaking point once my drinking entered the picture. The breakup was inevitable. They would urge me to stop drinking and seek help for my drinking, but I truly couldn't bear the thought of giving up alcohol. As foolish as it sounds, I felt that alcohol was my best friend—we had been through so much together. Alcohol was always there for me, it never showed up late, never sold me out for someone else, always promised to cheer me up, never cheated on me, and always made me feel good—at least for a little while. I didn't realize at the time that alcohol was robbing from me the entire time and enslaving me to its allure. And its consequences.

After coming to grips with my problem, I thought I could simply control my alcohol consumption. I tried to exercise more power over myself than the bottle possessed. When that failed, I tried to establish control measures to limit my drinking. I told myself things like, "Rather than drinking until you black out this coming Friday, why not just drink a six-pack and a bottle of wine?" That sounded like a reasonable plan to me; the only problem was that by the time the six-pack and the wine were gone, it was only 7 p.m., with plenty of evening still remaining.

I tried to hold out, but by 8 p.m., I was overcome by an irresistible urge to go down to the corner store for more alcohol. Having caved, I would come back with my arms full of beer, wine, cheap champagne, and snack food. I made sure to buy enough alcohol on those secondary trips because I knew that once I got into the booze, I'd be too impaired to safely go out to get any more.

I came to dread the urge to drink. I would try to fight it with all the willpower and Marine Corps discipline that I could muster, and I would always lose. Perhaps straight willpower works for some, but not for me. The urge to drink had become ingrained. If a person wears a watch on their wrist often enough, to forget it one day will cause an uncomfortable tugging sensation in their brain that something is off.

My urge to drink was the same kind of feeling, only more intense. The sensation reminded me of a time during my childhood where my brothers and I helped a neighbor with her farm animals. She had broken her leg, so we helped her feed and water her animals and change the electric fences around the pasture. One day, I was moving a section of electric fence and my brother turned on the juice. The pain from the electric shock wasn't hot and sharp, but rather strong and pulsing. When I was craving alcohol, a similar strong and pulsing sensation turned on in my brain.

By that point, I'd been drinking heavily for nine years, so the compulsion to drink was overwhelming when the weekend came around. I would fight the feeling all during the week, but as Friday approached I would become more and more anxious. Because as hard as I fought the urge, like every weekend before, I would find myself heading to the liquor store after work to stock up.

The battle I was beginning to fight with alcohol led me to try some offensive tactics. I tried hiding alcohol around the house so I wouldn't get to it, or at least, to curb my intake. In moments of resolve, I poured extra beer down the drain, I hid my car keys so I couldn't drive to the store, and I even tried hiding my wallet so that I couldn't buy more alcohol later on in the evening. None of it worked long-term. I found the alcohol and my wallet, I stopped pouring booze down the drain or simply bought more, and rather than driving, I just walked down to the corner store.

If I had a special occasion or an event to attend over the weekend, I could fight to stay sober on Friday, but by Saturday afternoon, the compulsion was so strong that I couldn't deny it any longer. The urge to drink would be screaming into my brain and the only way to make it go away was get some alcohol and drink it. I became so discouraged and sad over my lack of ability to control the monster inside that I didn't know where to turn. That's when God nudged me, and I finally listened.

That spring, my roommate started a men's Bible study in our house on Tuesday nights. Naturally, he invited me to attend and out of a sense of guilt and obligation, I agreed. I had attended church with him when I first got to Jacksonville, but since I no longer attended the church I felt that I owed him, so I attended his Bible study. We used the *Discovering God* workbook, and we watched a video each week and then discussed our coursework. We all took turns sharing. I felt the Holy Spirit convict me of my drinking and I actually began to open up to the guys. I had never shared with anyone about my drinking before, at least not past the surface level. I was afraid they would look down on me, but they listened with support and tried to encourage me.

Even though I continued to drink on the weekends, I was thankful for those guys. I began to develop a conscience and sense of guilt and shame over my sin, and I began to seek God's help and forgiveness. Towards the end of the Bible study, I made a resolution that I wasn't going to drink anymore. I was terrified of giving my commitment a voice with my men's group, because once the bell was wrung, it couldn't be undone. I would be held accountable. But, with God's help, I did voice my decision and the guys prayed for me. I felt so good about it that I was able to put the bottle away for over a month. A month might not seem like much time to be sober, but for me, it felt like a lifetime.

By mid-spring of 2009, I was given orders to report to Headquarters Marine Corps in Washington D.C., where I was to work in a staff officer capacity. I was excited about this opportunity. It was a chance for me to network and build myself professionally, but it was also an opportunity to start over. After four and a half years in Jacksonville, I felt that I'd worn that option out. I wanted a new start with new people in a new place, especially with my newly sober status. I had enjoyed living in the D.C. area during Officer Candidate School at Quantico and during my six months in The Basic School, so I was glad for the assignment.

I received the orders in April and I had one month to close out my life in Jacksonville and report for duty. I put a renter's deposit on a condo in Alexandria, Virginia that I found through a military website. Then I began the process of checking out of my command at Camp Lejeune, packing all my personal belongings, and arranging a truck to transport everything to the D.C. area. Because I had been sober for a month straight, I was well rested and confident about the move and starting over. Little did I know that within two months of moving north, I would again be heading down the path to heavy drinking.

10

I t was now May 2009, and I packed up my belongings and drove north to Washington D.C. to report to my new command at Headquarters Marine Corps. I had just enough of my one-month transition time remaining to move in and get all of my furniture and possessions situated in my new condo before I had to report to my new command.

My new place was a second story, two-bedroom condo with hardwood floors and plenty of space. It was located near my old stomping grounds on the western edge of King Street, the main street in Old Town Alexandria, Virginia. The location was ideal for commuting to work, a great gym was located right across the street, and I was close to all the restaurants, theaters, and of course, many local bars. I was quite familiar with the area from a few years prior when I was a student at The Basic School, and I had partied hard in Old Town during that time. Even though alcohol was within easy access, I was still resolute at this point that I would not fall back into that lifestyle.

After I finished staging my new home, I put on my uniform and went to Henderson Hall to check in with my new command. Henderson Hall shares the same hill as Arlington

National Cemetery and overlooks the Pentagon, the Potomac
River, and many historical sites in Washington. The check-in
process took a week and then I began to settle into my new
responsibilities. My duties were a complete change from my
previous assignments in the Marine Corps. I felt comfortable
leading Marines in battle at both the tactical level and on
operational level deployments, but I was now serving the
Marine Corps at a higher and more strategic level.

To a Marine, the Tactical Level refers to being on the
ground, leading troops, and operating in a specific country.
The Operational Level is a broader theatre of warfare, such as
the Eastern Theatre or the Pacific Theatres during World War
II. Rather than local fighting, the Operational Level deals with
regions and entire campaigns. Finally, the Strategic Level deals
with enterprise-wise capabilities and decisions that have far-
reaching implications. The Chairmen of the Joint Chiefs,
Central Command, and Headquarters Marine Corps are all
at the strategic level. This is where decisions are made and
future policy is developed that will affect the uniformed
services for generations to come.

My new job was with Installations and Logistics
Command, which was the logistics element for Headquarters
Marine Corps. Much of my daily interactions took place with
senior officers who were shaping the future of the Marine
Corps. Instead of dodging bullets and working crazy long
hours on deployments, I had to figure out the murky waters of
military politics and protocol. I was confident about logistical
plans when I briefed senior officers, but it was still unnerving
at the same time. I felt so out of place that I wondered if I had
made a mistake in transferring to headquarters. But I couldn't
go back, so I decided to give it my best.

As I navigated the ins and outs of my new job during the
week, I decided that I needed to support my sober time by
filling up my weekends with graduate school. The Marine
Corps partnered with various universities and brought

professors to the bases on weekends to teach college courses. I enrolled in an MBA program through Boston University and jumped right in. The Marine Corps flew the professors down from Boston to teach the classes in person.

My course load was two classes a semester and we met every other weekend. On class weekends, we were in class all day on Saturday and Sunday. On the weekends that I wasn't in class, I was studying and doing homework. While I was not 100 percent alcohol-free, I was sober more often than not. I was working out every day and in the best shape of my life. I was getting more comfortable with my new job requirements. And now, I was pursuing my MBA. All in all, things were going well.

Shortly after arriving in Washington D.C., I decided to get back into the dating scene to look for a meaningful relationship. I had gotten into online dating in Jacksonville, but too often I ended up dating the wrong kind of girl. Although I wasn't exactly living out my own faith, I always sought out Christian girls. I held onto the faith I was raised with, and I knew what I valued deep down, even though I couldn't seem to get there myself. After the initial conversations with girls online, we would meet in person for dates. At first, I never drank alcohol on these dates. But after several dates, I felt that I could introduce wine into the mix, as long as she was having wine also. I told myself that I wasn't getting drunk and I wasn't doing anything foolish and that it was alright. It was just social drinking. I could handle it. And I did just that. I handled it. The drinking didn't get out of control at first.

Soon, a glass of wine on a Friday night date turned into a six-pack after I got home. I would feel guilty, but then I would go to bed and not have another drink for three weeks. Later, I would get a bottle of liquor and keep it in the cabinet in case I wanted a night cap one evening. Then it became a few night caps. It seemed that my tolerance had diminished somewhat during my drinking sabbatical, so I wanted to be careful with what I consumed. If I drank enough to warrant a hangover, the hangover still wouldn't be terribly bad and I wanted to keep it that way. As long as I had only consumed several drinks the night before, my Saturday morning run was going to be okay. So, I continued to "handle it" and temper my drinking as I worked my new job, pursued my MBA, and met girls online.

I met Amy in July 2009 and I fell hard for her. From our very first date, I was totally hooked. She was a tall brunette with a vivacious personality, funny, and devoted to following Christ. We hit it off right from the start and soon we were inseparable. We spent every weekend together and saw each other a few evenings a week. As our relationship deepened, I found that my drinking took a back seat. In retrospect, I still desired to drink, but I had a great distraction in Amy. I drank here and there, but Amy and I were just starting out, and I was able to keep my drinking under control and also hide any signs of my drinking past.

Overall, I was incredibly hopeful for the future. Everything was looking up. I had a wonderful girl in my life, I was getting along at my new job and my Marine Corps career was progressing nicely, I was pursuing my master's degree, and now, even my drinking issues seemed to be diminishing.

IN THE MIDST OF ALL THE GOOD THINGS GOING ON IN MY LIFE, my stutter continued to plague me. As an officer in the Marines, I had to brief superiors and subordinates constantly. In particular, my new job at Headquarters Marine Corps required a fair amount of public speaking, either in meetings, briefings, or teaching classes to fellow Marine officers and enlisted personnel. Because of that exposure, I had become even more painfully aware of how I sounded to others. My fear of stuttering would cause me to get nervous, my palms would sweat, and my heart rate would kick into overdrive.

I remember shortly after I arrived in Washington D.C., my boss and I were scheduled to attend a working group of twenty fellow officers and civilians. In these types of meetings, it is a military courtesy to go around the room and introduce yourself and say what department you represent. Sounds simple enough, but I knew that saying my name fluently would be close to impossible, let alone getting through the rest of my intro. I was stressing over the intro even before the meeting started. Then as it got closer and closer to my turn to speak, I became terrified and knew that I was going to trip all over my words.

When the spotlight turned onto the couple people right ahead of me, I experienced a full-out panic attack. My heart leapt through my chest, I began to hyperventilate, I got tunnel vision, and my throat locked shut. To this day, I don't know how I was able to squeak out my name, rank, and department. All I knew was that I was professionally humiliated. To the credit of everyone in the room, no one said anything or made any derogatory comments, but I tortured myself by thinking about what must be going through their minds. That experience only reinforced my negative self-image. It seemed like confirmation of what I had been telling myself my entire life, that I was broken and damaged. Even the Marine Corps didn't fully fix it.

In September of that year, I received some help for my stutter from an unexpected source. Shortly after I checked into my command, I was scheduled to participate in a meet-and-greet with our commanding general. Of course, I was nervous. I was a captain and could handle interactions with other captains and majors and even lieutenant colonels, but conversing one-on-one with a general? That was outside the realm of comfort.

Generals were a rare species of Marine that we heard

about with awe in stories, or maybe we got a glimpse of one from across the parade deck. At that point in my career, the thought of actually sitting down with a general scared me to death. But the day came for the meeting and when I knocked on the general's door, he invited me in and we sat down at his table and began to chat. He was a pleasant man and after ten or fifteen minutes, our interaction finished. It wasn't all that bad, but I still breathed easier when it was over.

The following day, I was sitting at my desk minding my own business when I felt a hand drop on my shoulder. I turned around and there he was, the general, standing right behind me. I started to bolt to my feet out of respect but he lightly pushed me back down into my chair and then pulled another chair over and took a seat next to me. He motioned me closer so that our heads were nearly touching and told me that he had also been born with a stutter and that it had plagued him early on in his career as well. He told me about a chaplain who had referred him to a specialist, and the general now wanted to help me as well.

I was a little embarrassed to have my stutter noticed by the general, but I also felt immensely grateful at the same time. I had come across only a few people in my life with a stutter, but never another Marine, let alone a general officer. It was comforting to know that I wasn't the only officer in the Marine Corps with a speech impediment. After so many years of feeling self-conscious, it also gave me some hope. If another Marine with a stutter could attain the rank of general, then why couldn't I potentially do the same?

The general put me in touch with the same chaplain who had helped him years before. As only God could arrange, the chaplain had stayed in the Navy and was actually working in the same building as the general and myself. I went to see the chaplain and he set me up with the same medical specialist he had referred the general to see all those years before. And doubly remarkable, the specialist also worked in the same building as the rest of us. Breaking from my past experiences with speech pathologists, this specialist was a medical doctor with some special training in ear, nose, and throat (ENT) cases.

He examined me and prescribed some anti-depressant medication to help regulate my mood and take away the underlying anxiety of speaking in public. He also gave me a referral to Walter Reed Hospital for a special ear device to be molded and customized for me that helps to manage stuttering. I couldn't put into words how grateful I was. The medication immediately began to help me speak fluently. I still stuttered, but it was now occasional rather than every other sentence and I had far more control over it. The ear device also gradually trained my ear to hear my own voice and other sounds differently, which helped me speak more smoothly. I found myself actually beginning to enjoy speaking in public.

Even though these things were helping my stutter, I soon found out that one of the side effects of the anti-depressant medication was an increased response to the effects of alcohol. I'll never forget the day when I mixed my anti-depressant medication and booze for the first time. I had been itching to drink again, so I waited for a weekend when Amy was out of town visiting her family. I drank most of a bottle of scotch on Friday night and when I woke up the next day, rather than being hung over, I was still drunk. I had no idea what had happened to me. The drunk feeling had never lingered like this before, not ever.

I drank water and coffee and went for a jog, but I didn't sober up until later that evening. I finally put together what must have happened in terms of the medication combined with alcohol.

I didn't know how I was going to keep drinking now, and I was distressed that my secret was going to come out. Foolishly, I wasn't worried about the medical side effects of mixing medication with alcohol. After all, I didn't think it would kill me. No, I was simply worried about how long the recovery process would take. Because even if I wanted to curtail my drinking, I knew I would cave eventually, and even binge drink. So how could I keep my drinking from Amy if the after-effects lasted that long? I couldn't expect to carry on a relationship with Amy and be drunk from Friday to Sunday night.

I realized I would have to rearrange my whole schedule in order to carry on my drinking habit and still take the medication. Instead of deciding to leave drinking behind, my solution was to become crafty with alcohol. I had never been crafty before. I just drank and let people deal with it as they chose. Now, a new element began to manifest in my life... *deceit*.

Keeping a relationship with alcohol and keeping a relationship with Amy at the same time took enormous effort. I wasn't drinking often, but when I did, I had to get creative to conceal it. If I drank one Friday night, I had to make up a lie as to why I couldn't see her that night, plus I would have to make up another lie so that I could recover all day on Saturday. I had to ignore phone calls and be sure to text her only, and only text when I was first drinking and still relatively clear-headed. Any later than that and I might say something nonsensical once I was drunk.

I had to live a double life and it became hard to remember what lie went with what scenario I had created, but keeping the stories straight was critical. It didn't take long before I began to get the sense that I had two girlfriends, Amy and alcohol, and the only way to be with one was to cheat on the other. Coming to terms with that notion was hard for me. Had I really sunk to the place where I had to choose one or the other? Had I reached such a low point in my life that I would even contemplate the choice between a real relationship or one with alcohol? The answer was yes and yes, and acknowledging my true relationship with alcohol was the start of my self-loathing. I would look in the mirror and be disgusted with myself, but it still didn't motivate me to change.

I was able to maintain the double life for several months, but a chink in my armor happened in October of 2009. It was a Friday evening and Amy was going to come over for dinner. I arrived home from work around 4 p.m. and worked out heavily at the gym across the street from my condo. After cleaning up, I drove several blocks up the street to get groceries for dinner. While browsing the aisles, I called her and asked if she wanted me to pick up a bottle of wine. We were having Italian for dinner and I thought it would be nice to have a glass of wine with the meal. She thought it was a great idea, so I purchased two bottles of wine. The deceit that was building in me knew full well that I had no intention of having just one or two glasses of wine. Even though it wasn't a conscious decision, my deceitful side was fully planning on a lot more wine than that.

As I left the grocery store, the strong alcohol urges I'd been placating for months hit my brain hard. It totally shocked me because the overwhelming desire seemingly came out of nowhere, and I couldn't ignore it this time. In fact, my heart began to race and my breath quickened the more I tried not to think about alcohol. Before I could wrap my mind around what I was doing, I was at the liquor store on the corner of the strip mall next to the grocery purchasing a pint of vodka. I was ashamed of myself for succumbing, but I shrugged it off and drove home. I got the groceries inside and began to prepare dinner.

Amy was still an hour or so away from arriving, so I mixed myself a drink of vodka and cherry coke. A pint of vodka can mix about five drinks. By the time Amy arrived, I had mixed and drank all five drinks. I worried that she would see the empty pint bottle and become upset, so I hid the empty bottle. I couldn't put it in the trash because that would be obvious. I couldn't put it in a cupboard, because what if she went looking for a dish or pan and found it? I couldn't hide it in the coat closet because what if she needed to hang something up? I had a strong buzz coming on and decided I needed to hide it where she would never think to look. I went into my guest bathroom, took the top off of the toilet tank, and sank the bottle to the bottom.

Amy arrived shortly after the deed was done. As we poured glasses of wine while we finished the meal preparations, she began to notice that my behavior was changing. She questioned me about it; I must have tipped her off by laughing too hard at her jokes or saying something edgy. She asked if I had consumed something else in addition to the wine, as one or two glasses was not enough to intoxicate someone of my physical size. She was exactly right, but I blew off her questioning. I wasn't going to admit to drinking all that vodka and she couldn't prove it. Dinner was strained, and afterwards as we were sitting down to watch a movie, she flat out accused me of lying to her. She became more furious as I continued my denial.

I left the room briefly and when I came back, she was gone. I figured she had bailed, so I raced down to the parking garage and she was just pulling out of my guest slot. I flagged her down and begged her to stay. She was so mad that she almost floored the gas pedal and blew past me, but she stopped and rolled her window down. I still didn't admit that I drank all the vodka. Instead, I blamed it on my medication, another lie. Well, a half-lie. As she saw the anxiousness in my face, she softened and told me that she would see me the next day. I felt sorrow, not because I had lied to her, but because she'd almost found out about my embarrassing love affair with alcohol.

After she left, I went back upstairs and poured the remaining wine into a glass and drank it all. At that point it was only 9 p.m. and I could legally buy alcohol for another three hours. I changed out of my jeans and dress shirt and jumped into more relaxing gym clothes, put on my shoes, and walked down to the corner store. I came home with an 18-pack and cracked the beer as soon as I entered my condo. I finally passed out on my couch around 1 a.m.

I woke up at 11 a.m. the next day, still drunk due to the medication. I knew that I had to see Amy that night to try and make things right, so I put on my gym clothes and jogged down the block to my gym. I spent about three hours lifting weights, doing cardio, and sweating it out in the sauna.

By 7 p.m., enough of the alcohol had burned off and I was sober again. Amy came back that evening and I asked for her forgiveness. She was such a sweetheart that she forgave me willingly. The regret and shame had been building in me all day long, and I felt real remorse for what I had done, but I still couldn't confess the truth to her. I thanked her for her forgiveness and I resolved in my heart not to drink again, or at least for a long while.

After that episode, I was able to maintain sobriety for a month, but it was a struggle each day. I began to feel like a fish out of water trying to survive in an environment that wasn't made for me. To deny alcohol was like living underwater and holding my breath. Sooner or later I absolutely had to come up for air. I just had to.

Within a month, my propensity to abuse alcohol was reestablishing itself, Amy or no Amy. The urge to drink would build and continue building until I couldn't deny the screaming in my brain any longer. I started the work week on Monday and each time, the resolution was the same. I would say to myself with all the fresh resolve and discipline I could muster, "I will not drink, I will not drink, I will not drink." Early in the week I could resist the urge, but as Thursday came around, the claws would dig into my brain. Then Friday would hit and the claws would dig in more viciously with each passing hour.

After hitting the gym on Friday afternoon, I would start to

head home, but then inevitably I would find myself turning towards the the liquor store. A short while later, I would be leaving with alcohol in-hand, thinking to myself, "Now, how did that happen?" It was as if I was moving in a trance or in some of kind of out-of-body experience. I always felt a disgusted kind of wonderment that I could resist all week and ultimately still give in on Friday. As soon as I got home and began to drink, the mental urge wouldn't vanish. Instead, it would change form. The urge to drink transformed into an urge to *not run out of alcohol*.

Someone once said to me, "One drink is too many and one hundred is not enough." Once I tasted that first drink, I had no choice but to drink and drink until blackout.

11

My drinking had never singled handedly destroyed a personal relationship for me. To be sure, I had lost friendships and short-lived romances because of drinking, but none that I truly cared about. That all changed on New Year's Eve 2009.

By then, I was head over heels for Amy. We had weathered the storm that I caused back in October due to my drinking. She had stuck by me, and I'd been able to conceal my drinking just enough. We had shared Thanksgiving at her parent's house and then exchanged Christmas gifts. I warmed to the idea of a marriage proposal in the near future, but all of that changed after New Year's Eve.

Several weeks before the holiday, we discussed how we might want to celebrate the New Year. In a rather convenient twist, I thought it would be great to attend a themed New Year's Eve party being hosted by the church we both attended. The theme was going to be the roaring 20's and costumes were encouraged. It sounded fun, but also appealing because it would be a no-booze party to usher in the New Year. I figured I would be safe from the urge to drink while in Amy's company.

We settled on the 1920's party to celebrate, but then the plans changed. Amy's best friend and other college friends decided to come to D.C. for New Year's Eve and they wanted to go out on the town and party instead. Nervously, I agreed to go along with the second option, even though I had a feeling of foreboding. It was like I knew that something bad would happen to us, or me, if we went out for a wild party.

Once the decision to go out on the town was made, we shopped around for clubs that offered a flat fee for all you could eat and drink. We settled on a club in Clarendon, Virginia that was halfway between my house and Amy's house. The tickets were expensive, but I figured that we would make up the value based on the amount of food and drinks that we consumed. Amy's friends arrived several days before New Year's Eve and the girls spent several days catching up together.

On New Year's Eve, I drove to Amy's house to finish getting ready for our night out. The girls were already there, putting on their makeup and dresses, totally having a great time. Once everyone was ready, we gathered in the living room for pictures and a toast of champagne. By that time, the sense of foreboding was gone and I was looking forward to enjoying the evening. When it was time to head to the club, I called cabs for everyone and we piled in. It was still early in the evening, only 9 p.m., and the club had just opened its doors.

The club expected a packed house that night, but since it was still early, we were able to get a great table right next to the buffet. As more and more people began to arrive, dinner was served and the bar opened. It was an open bar, but customary to tip the bartenders. I started to get a little nervous. An open bar meant I could drink as much as I wanted and it would only cost me tips. I quickly pulled myself together and vowed to stay sober… at least *relatively* sober.

At first, I stayed true to my intentions and took it easy on the drinks. After a couple rounds, I began to feel calmer, more collected. *I've got this,* I thought to myself. The truth is that the alcohol was seeping into me, whispering sweet nothings to my mind, fooling me into thinking I was in total control.

Two drinks became three, and three became six. Amy was constantly being distracted by her girlfriends. They would want to dance, or go outside for a while, or whatever. Each of those distractions provided me with an excellent opportunity to swing by the bar for another drink without her knowing. Ironically, Amy was repeatedly asking me to take it easy on the booze that night. The October incident was still in the back of her mind, and she didn't want the evening getting ruined by me drinking too much alcohol. I should have listened to her, but my other girlfriend, alcohol, was uppermost in my thoughts that night.

By 11 p.m., the alcohol had suppressed the food in my system and I was already drunk. Amy whisked me out onto the dance floor and I hoped that I could burn some of it off before she realized how much I had already consumed. I was more than a little unsteady on my feet and I was wondering if I could even keep my balance on the dance floor. Lucky for me, the dance floor was so packed that I barely had enough space to rock back and forth on my feet. At least the crowd would keep me from falling all over myself in an attempt to dance. However, I had consumed too much and by the time the ball dropped at midnight, I was past the point of no return. I was totally drunk.

I managed to kiss Amy at midnight and then headed to the bar to get another round of drinks for all of us. Shortly after 1 a.m., Amy came back from the bathroom and said she was looking for one of her friends. Her friend had drunk entirely too much, and after some searching we found her passed out, sitting on a chair, propped up in the corner in the coat room. Amy was completely sober and had the presence of mind to get her girlfriend out of the party. She wanted me to leave also. Amy flat-out said that I'd had enough booze and that we needed to take care of her friend. But of course, I wanted to stay and keep drinking. It was an open bar, after all, and what a waste leaving early would be.

Begrudgingly, I told Amy that I needed to use the bathroom first before leaving, so I went downstairs to the men's room. I came back up after a few minutes and instead of heading outside, I took a detour by the bar and pounded two more drinks as fast as I could. Then, I stumbled outside to meet Amy on the street, but she was not there. I assumed she and her friend had decided that they couldn't wait on me and left on their own, figuring that I would follow in my own cab.

Instead of getting my coat and hailing a cab to follow them home, I went back inside, got another drink at the bar, and looked for Amy's friends to see what they were up to then. Because it was late and dark and I was drunk, I couldn't find them. In my inebriated state, I thought that the girls had ditched me and of course, Amy had left me at the party also. I became annoyed. I went to the coat room for my overcoat, hailed a cab, and told the driver to take me to my house. I had totally forgotten that my car was still parked in Amy's driveway. I didn't even have my apartment keys with me.

As I rode along in the cab, my phone began to ring. It was Amy. In my anger and frustration, I kept directing the calls to voice mail. Amy was trying to find out where I was and if I was okay. After the twenty-minute cab ride, I was dropped off in front of the gate to my community. I paid the cab driver and staggered up the walkway to my building. I didn't have my keys or my door entry fob, so I figured I would have to go down into the parking garage, come up through the service entrance and use a credit card to pick the lock on my condo door. That was my very last thought before I blacked out.

I woke up the next morning in a crumpled heap in front of my locked condo door. I lived on the third floor and somehow, I had gotten inside my building. I looked at my watch and it was 5 a.m. The knees of my trousers were ripped and my palms were bloody, and there were leaves and pine needles in my pockets. Blood? Pine needles? What in the world had happened? I was still drunk, but I managed to take a credit card from my pocket and jimmy the door so that I could get inside.

Once inside, I turned on the light and noticed that there was a handwritten note on my dining room table. I was in no condition to read the note, so I just turned off the light and literally fell into bed. I woke up again later that morning, around 11 a.m., still slightly drunk. As I got up from bed, I felt the bruises on my body where I'd torn up my hands and knees. Gingerly, I walked into the dining room and noticed the note on the table again. I finally checked and saw the note was from Amy.

Amy? How did she get in my house to leave me a note without stepping over me, collapsed in a drunken stupor at my front door? I colored as I envisioned the sight and what the thoughts of passers-by must have been, seeing me crumpled in a drunken heap outside my door. But even though I was embarrassed, I didn't think Amy had found me last night. Even though I had no memory of the night's events after getting out of the cab, I tried to piece together what must have happened.

When I left the cab to walk down to the parking garage the night before, I must have fallen into the bushes and blacked out, hence the bloodied palms, torn clothes, and all the leaves. After getting her friend home, Amy had used my keys to drive my car to my condo to look for me and didn't notice me passed out in the bushes. She then must have used my keys to gain entry to my condo, wrote the note for me and left, and then I had come-to enough to crawl out of the bushes and up to my door before passing out again outside.

Having pieced the scenario together, I finally read Amy's note and could hear the unbridled fury in her voice. She was done with me. She accused me of purposely blowing off her wishes to stay sober, getting drunk instead, and going home with another girl. She had assumed this after I didn't respond to her texts, and after searching my condo and finding no trace of me. Of course, I had not gone home with another girl, but had I done anything less repulsive? Not really.

All that day I felt sub-human. I was wracked by guilt and shame and felt such sorrow for losing Amy. I had no doubt we were over. All for what, a dozen free drinks at a bar? At long last, my cheating on Amy with alcohol had forced its way into the spotlight, and my true love, alcohol, had demanded a terrible price.

Later that evening, once I was sober, I began the six-mile walk to Amy's house. No matter what was to become of us, I had to retrieve my keys and car and try to make things right. The outside temperature was about 25 degrees, so I wrapped myself up in a heavy fleece and began jogging towards her house. I needed to punish myself and I wasn't going to take the easy way out and call a cab. A six-mile run through the freezing night air was what I deserved.

All along the way I was thinking of what I would say when I saw her. Should I try to talk my way out of it? Maybe downplay what really happened? My usual method of damage control was to fast-talk my way out of things, but I knew it wouldn't work this time. I decided that I would just be honest with her and let her decide.

When I was a mile or two away, I was so cold that I broke down and sent her a text, and she came to pick me up. We pulled into her driveway and just sat there, looking at each other. What could I possibly say to her? *I'm sorry?* It wouldn't cut it this time. In a torrent of emotion, I began to apologize and confess my wrongs to her about my drinking the night before. She just looked at me with her arms crossed. She wasn't buying any of my explanations.

After an hour of pleading, I could see that she was still hardened against me, and I began to cry. With tears pouring down my cheeks, in all sincerity, I began to weep. For her, for myself, for my life, and for everything I had done. That finally broke her resolve. There I was, a 6'4", 250-pound muscular and toughened United States Marine Corps officer, and I was weeping like a child.

She put her arms around me and held me close and asked me if I was truly sorry. I said yes, and she forgave me and kissed me and told me that it was ok and she wouldn't leave me. Oh, the relief and joy that flooded my body! I couldn't believe it. At that moment, I resolved in my heart to change my ways and be worthy of the love of this incredible woman. I promised her that I would never drink again, and in that moment, I actually believed it.

With 2010 underway, I was resolute that I would stay sober and leave the drinking behind me. I was still reeling from the events that surrounded New Year's Eve, and I truly did want to be better, at least for Amy if not for myself. I didn't have a drink for several weeks, and Amy and I started taking timid steps to rebuild our relationship.

She had forgiven me, yes, but reconciliation was going to take some work. I had broken her trust and hurt her deeply. I was determined to make it up to her. While my intentions were pure, to quit drinking and be good to Amy, my methods and resolve were flawed and bound to fail. I still was not ready to turn my life over to God's leading.

Truth is, I had become somewhat resentful towards God. As my drinking worsened over the years, I would pray to God and ask for deliverance, thinking that surely God would hear my earnest cry and help me. Because God *does* hear our cries. The problem was that my words in the moment didn't reflect any sort of lasting heart change. Instead, they were the reactive uttering of a few magic words, as if I could hocus-pocus myself out of jail free and clear whenever the crisis hit. I wanted God to fix my mess whenever things got beyond my realm of control, but then I would go back to my old ways when the crisis was averted.

Even though my pleading with God could be heartfelt and real in the moment, there was still part of me deep down that didn't want to give up the reins of my life to Him. I thought a simple prayer should be all that it took; that I should be released from the desire to drink since surely, that must be what God wanted for me also. I would say to myself, *I have prayed and prayed and prayed some more that God would take away my problem with alcohol, so why hasn't He done it yet?* And the more I couldn't seem to stop drinking, the angrier I got.

My reasoning was that because I wanted to change, at least on a surface level, God owed it to me to make it so. My troubled thoughts were murmuring accusations of God's betrayal. *Does God even care about what I am going through? Here I am crying out to Him over the years that I want Him to change me, and I am not getting anything in return. What is the point of trying to serve Him if He is just going to turn His back on me and let me keep wallowing in my sin?*

Even though I had grown up in the church and had gotten saved at an early age, I really didn't know much about living a fulfilled Christian life. More importantly, I didn't understand the *source* of the fulfillment we're supposed to have as Christians. Rather, I went through the motions. I had been brought up in Sunday school and youth group and I'd attended a Christian college with regular chapel services on campus. I knew all the Bible stories and the pat Christian responses to life's ups and downs. I'd even sought out churches to attend throughout my Marine Corps career, although it was sometimes on a nominal basis. Despite these efforts at living the Christian life, my heart still knew little of what it really meant to have a relationship with God. I certainly didn't live out my faith or act all that differently from people around me. The idea of "getting right with God" was always something that I figured I would do later.

Reflecting back, I realize that God was reaching out to me so many times, but I was the one that didn't have the motivation or heart to respond. Even the church I attended with Amy was heavily focused on the Bible and had many opportunities to connect with other believers, but I just wasn't all that interested in getting connected. I didn't have any ill will towards the idea or church activities, but life seemed to always get in the way or I had other priorities. There was always a "later." At least, that was the case until Amy told me that I needed to join a men's group for some devoted Bible study and godly relationships at our church. The way she *asked* me to join a group didn't leave much room for doubt. She was telling me that if I wanted her in my life, I had better do as she said.

So, I joined a Christian men's small group at our church. I figured that digging into the Bible and being accountable to a men's small group couldn't hurt; it would keep Amy in my life and perhaps it would even give me the necessary courage and power to turn over a new leaf. Indeed, I found that the men's small group was covering good content, but it wasn't the quick fix I was seeking. I still wasn't interested in doing the hard work of changing my behavior or giving God complete ownership over my life.

I loved to drink. I didn't want to give it up, simple as that.

So many people around me drank all the time, and they didn't seem to struggle with negative consequences. Why couldn't God allow me that ability? Why couldn't I drink like other people and keep it together? What I really wanted was for God to let me keep drinking, but magically take away the negative consequences of my actions. Complete foolishness, of course, but that is what my heart wanted. I kept hoping that God would eventually help me figure out how to manage my drinking.

I struggled to stay sober through January, but towards the end of the month it became more and more difficult. The desire to get drunk was always in the back of my mind. My mind would even rationalize my desire to drink until I reached a point when I believed I deserved to indulge myself in drinking and that it was good for me. So, it was only a matter of time before my thoughts turned into action and I picked up the bottle again.

It was now February, and the area got pounded with some heavy snowfall. Because of snowdrifts bordering on 5 feet, rare for Northern Virginia, the government shut down and so did the local military bases. Amy still had to work, but I didn't. Gloriously, I found myself holed up in my condo because of the snow for two or three days with no one to see and nothing to do but drink alcohol, and that is precisely what I did.

I will never forget that second day of the base being shut down due to the snow. It was about 4 p.m. and Amy had finished working for the day and was out sledding in the snow. She called me to see what I was up to with my day. By then, I was deep into a twenty-four pack of beer, and stupidly, I answered the phone. My speech was slurred and she picked up on it right away. I am sure the first thing that raced through her mind was that she had been a fool for taking me back into her life. We ended that phone call on very unpleasant terms, but the relationship wasn't over yet. We hung on for another two weeks, and then Amy came over one night for dinner.

As we finished eating, she told me that she thought we needed to take a break for one month. She told me that I had hurt her and that she needed time away from me to sort out how she felt. She proposed that we not see or speak to each other for one month, and then get back together and assess where we were. I kept quite a poker face, but inside I was hurt and glad and disgusted all at the same time. Hurt that she would want to stay away from me, but glad that I could spend time with my other girlfriend, alcohol, and not have to worry about covering my tracks. And then as soon as that thought crossed my mind, disgust followed right behind. *What was I thinking? Was I really happy about giving Amy up and drinking instead? Really? What was wrong with me?* I went ahead and agreed with Amy about taking the break. There was nothing else I could say or do. As she left, I put my arms around her and kissed her. I told her that I loved her and that I would see her in a month.

Instead of using that month to get my life together, I went on a one-month bender. I kept it together for work, but I now had free rein to drink on the weekends with no thought of a girlfriend to temper my habits. I was no longer accountable to Amy, and I also skipped church because I didn't want to be prompted to take a long, hard look at my choices. Instead, I would get home from work on Friday afternoon and immediately go to the gym, then head to the store for food and drinks to last me through the weekend. I bought enough alcohol upfront to keep me busy until Sunday afternoon—two cases of beer, a bottle of scotch, often a bottle of wine as well. I figured that whatever I couldn't drink by Sunday afternoon could be kept for the following weekend.

During that month-long separation, I drank myself further and deeper than ever before. Even my demeanor at the office was different. I never showed up to work drunk, but coming off those weekend benders was impossible to do in a day. In fact, it would take a few days for me to begin to function normally. That much alcohol took days to oxidize out of my system.

On Monday, my eyes were bloodshot, my breathing labored, and my reflexes out of sync. By Tuesday, my breath was still short, but my reflexes were better. By Wednesday, I felt almost myself again. By Thursday, the self-loathing and shame had set in and I was promising myself that I would not drink that weekend. By Friday afternoon, I was heading to the liquor store. The pattern always repeated. My co-workers and my boss never said anything to me during that month, but I'm sure they could tell something was amiss. My men's group and Amy were really the only solid Christian influences that I had in my life, and with her absent, I had virtually no restraint left. I was still connected to the men's group, but since I didn't confide in them 100%, they couldn't help me.

The month apart went by fast. I missed Amy, but I had so much distraction in drinking that it breezed by. We got together again around the middle of March to discuss our relationship and where we wanted it to go. I was totally unprepared for what she said to me. I thought she was going to say that she wanted to move on, that I was a loser, and that she deserved better than me. That's what she should have said. Instead, she told me that she loved me and that she wanted us to work out.

I couldn't believe it. A secret part of me wanted her to walk away for good. If she did that, I could keep on drinking. If she stayed, then I would have to come to terms with myself and clean up my life. I wasn't sure I was ready for that. In fact, I knew I wasn't ready for that, but I went along with Amy in the moment because it felt better than the alternative of a true breakup.

≈

IF AMY AND I HAD A TOUGH RECONCILIATION AFTER NEW

Year's Eve, then we had a very fragile truce now. I knew she would be watching me closely, looking for any signs of drinking or lies. Any breach of her trust would result in her walking away from me forever. I cared about her and I aspired to be worthy, but it felt like I was under the microscope all the time. Indeed, the struggle to live up to what she wanted proved to be too much.

The reckoning took place in April. Amy had plans to go up to New York City with some of her girlfriends for the weekend to celebrate her birthday. I offered to let her have her girl time and stay home, but the truth is that she didn't even invite me for her birthday weekend.

While she was gone, I made the deliberate decision to get drunk. I think part of me wanted some closure to the relationship and I couldn't muster the courage to tell Amy that it was over between us. I mean, why would I? She was pretty, a Christian, a real sweetheart, she didn't have a deceitful or cruel bone in her body, and she loved me. What man in his right mind would turn that down? But I was so turned around in my thinking that I wanted alcohol more than I wanted her. I was even starting to resent her because I couldn't drink alcohol freely and do whatever I wanted.

Even though I wanted the breakup, I couldn't bring myself to speak the truth to her, to tell her that I actually wanted her to leave me so that I could drink freely. The only way that I could make it happen was to let her catch me in the act of drinking. To do that would mean lowering myself even further in her eyes, willfully turning my back on her and our relationship, and taking the cowardly way out. I couldn't bring myself to end the relationship, so I had to drive her to end it instead.

This was common ground for me. I was all too familiar with the feeling of being a complete loser and having people look down on me. I had found myself on the bottom rung of things all throughout high school. Drinking became the means to navigate and survive college. Then I drank throughout all my years in the Marines as a way to self-medicate how I viewed myself, so I was now fully at home in my drunken lifestyle. What was one more debasement?

Amy called me after her second night in New York City. I knew that she would, and I answered the phone even though I had already been drinking that evening. After we exchanged a few pleasantries and I inquired about her trip, the inevitable happened. She asked me if I had been drinking. I said that I had not. She knew that was a lie of course, because she could *hear* the alcohol in my voice. She began to cry and told me that she deserved better than me and that she couldn't do this to herself anymore. Her heart was just too broken.

Immediately I countered with promises of sobriety and reform, but they were hollow and empty. Even though I had intentionally done it, to end it, I was still experiencing the fight mentality. Second-guessing myself and trying to hold on, rather than lose something I would regret in the morning. After several minutes of back and forth, she became silent and with tears in her voice she said, "Goodbye, Jordan." Then she quietly hung up the phone.

I sat on my couch and vacantly stared at my bookcases without seeing anything. The alcohol in my system was making it difficult to think and I struggled to clear my head. How was I supposed to react? I had chosen this, but was I supposed to be happy or sad or indifferent? After a wave of regret, I felt relief that the struggle to be worthy of her was over. I even felt some sense of rightness, that she really did deserve better than me and at least I had done the right thing by her. Waves of shame were also hitting me because I realized I had just lost the best girl to ever come into my life.

I had cared about Amy so much, but I had also messed it up in epic proportions. No woman wants to compete with alcohol for first place standing. How crazy was I for choosing alcohol? Sooner or later my love for alcohol and my true self always came to light. All the rest that I presented to people was just a charade.

I wasn't ready to dwell on the shame or guilt over my behavior, so I let alcohol re-muddle my thoughts. I got up off of the couch and went to the refrigerator to crack open another beer, drowning out everything else.

12

After Amy broke things off with me, I descended even lower than where I had been before. I merely existed during the week until the weekend arrived and I could drink again. During weekends, I didn't attend church, I didn't go to the gym, and I didn't see any of my friends. My days away from the office consisted of nothing but sitting on my couch, drinking, and binging on junk food. Somehow, I clung onto enough discipline to make it through my Marine Corps duties. I felt like the Marine Corps was the only thing I had left, and I didn't dare mess that up. But weekends? That was my time to do whatever I wanted.

The drinking only partially masked what I felt during the difficult months following the breakup. Even though I told myself that losing Amy was a good thing, deep down, I knew better. I finally had to face the fact that alcohol had cost me someone that I deeply cared about, a girl that I loved.

As I began to acknowledge my actions, the shame and guilt were overwhelming. What was wrong with me? Why did I continue to drink and do this to myself weekend after weekend? These feelings intensified as time wore on. The emotional havoc that I carried with me was such a burden on my spirit. I would look in the mirror and see a hollowed, drunken man staring back at me. My self-talk was always negative. *Jordan, you were born a loser and you will always be a loser. You might as well live like one.*

Self-punishment seemed to be what the doctor ordered, so I drank non-stop and beat myself up about it the entire time. Sometimes I played around with alcohol during the week, but never too much. I had too much to lose professionally, so I kept the drinking for the weekends and hated myself the whole time.

One Saturday afternoon in late May, I remember sitting on the couch, completely drunk, and reflecting how my life had turned out. The weather outside was warm and beautiful, and the door to my porch was open to let in the breeze. Professionally, I had accomplished a great deal. I held the rank of a Marine captain, traversed myself to war twice and back, and I excelled at my job. Personally, however, I was a total wreck. Except for training events with the Marines and deployment time, I hadn't been able to string together more than six sober weekends in nearly ten years.

That day, as the fresh air breezed into my condo, I remember asking God why He had made me such a loser. What was wrong with me? I received no answer, but before long, tears were streaming down my cheeks. I looked to my right and saw my Bible laying on the end table. I picked it up and my Bible fell open to the Sermon on the Mount. I had nothing to lose, so why not read a little? My current path was leading me towards destruction and I knew that I needed to change. I was more than convinced at this point that I had absolutely no power to do so on my own. I was willing to admit my own sin and inability to control my addiction, and I knew that God held the answers that I was so desperate to find.

I spent the rest of that afternoon reading my Bible and eventually I started praying. I asked God for forgiveness and to help me with real change in my life. In the early evening, I worked up some courage and went to the refrigerator and poured the rest of my beer down the drain. Then I went back to reading the Bible and praying. As the evening wore on, I felt completely exhausted... spiritually, emotionally, and physically. I finally went to bed in the early hours of the morning.

The next day, I woke up hung over, but determined to stay sober. As I reflected on the emotions of the night before and my earnest prayer, I felt that I had finally been freed and that things would surely be easier now. God had "fixed" me, like one of the miraculous healings that Jesus did in the Bible. How little did I know that none of that was true.

I was forgiven, of course, but I still had not changed inside. I was too immature to understand that a few hours of praying and reading the Bible was a good start, but true change would come from completely surrendering my lifestyle to the Lord, day in and day out. For the moment, I was merely riding an emotional wave, and like all waves, they eventually crash.

IT WAS NOW JUNE OF 2010, AND I WAS SET TO BEGIN A MONTH-long advanced logistical school on Marine Corps Base Quantico. The class was a career enhancer and was designed for more senior officers such as majors and lieutenant colonels, but I had been offered a seat as a captain. After the first day of classes ended, I was driving back to my office when my cell phone rang. It was my boss, telling me that some new staffing requirements had just come down from Headquarters Marine Corps. I had been chosen for a one-year deployment to Kabul, Afghanistan and I needed to be overseas within the month.

A one-year deployment! I was quite happy with the news. I

had made such a mess of things recently that I relished the idea of focused time away, to use as a reset of sorts. I felt that God was giving me a chance to make some positive changes. The career benefits notwithstanding, I would be in an alcohol-free environment for an entire year and I could get myself together and have some real sober time under my belt without the opportunity to drink. In addition to sobriety, going overseas for a year to a joint command was an excellent career move. It would broaden my resume as an officer and almost guarantee me promotion to the rank of Major.

During the next few days, I was so busy getting ready to leave Virginia that I didn't have much time to drink. I did get hammered once or twice, but I kept it together for the most part. There was simply too much to do. I packed up my entire condo, put everything into long-term storage, and said goodbye to the few people who actually cared about what might happen to me.

Despite how things had ended with Amy, she had not completely shut me out. Officially we had broken up, but she occasionally called or texted me and said that she still cared about me. When I got the news that I was heading back to war, I wanted to share it with Amy. I felt confident that I would come back safe and in one piece, but there is never a 100 percent guarantee.

I called Amy the same day that I found out. We hadn't spoken in several weeks and she seemed glad to hear my voice. I then told her the news and she fell apart. She'd never had a relationship with someone who was going off to war and even though we were no longer together, she didn't know how to handle the news or what to think. She asked if she could see me before I left and I was touched. Even though I'd made a mess of things, it was nice to know that she appeared to still have feelings for me. We made plans for later in the week.

We met for dinner a few days later and talked. I didn't want to rehash all of the old wounds, so I tried to keep it positive. She had a hard time keeping her emotions together. I gave her a hug at the end, she promised to write me, and then we parted ways. She said that she'd continue to pray for me and that maybe a year away would be good for "us." Us? I didn't want to get my hopes up too much, but it felt good to know that perhaps we weren't completely finished after all.

Within two weeks, I was driving down to Camp Lejeune in Jacksonville, NC for two weeks of pre-deployment training. My younger brother, a fellow Marine officer who was also stationed at Camp Lejeune, allowed me to stay at his apartment while I waited to fly overseas. I finished my pre-deployment training in just a few days and then settled in to wait on my orders to come through so that I could fly to Afghanistan.

There wasn't anything for me to do on the base, but I had to call the office or send an email each morning to check in and give my whereabouts. Other than that, I was free to do as I wished. I would be flying to Kabul as soon as my security clearance was upgraded. In the meantime, I was stuck in Jacksonville until I met with the investigator and was cleared. It ended up being six weeks before I could fly out.

Even though God had arranged a way for me to find my way back to Him via a deployment, I soon forgot about His grace. Rather than remembering my prayer for forgiveness, or trying to make a change in my life, I fell back into my old ways at the first opportunity. I found myself with plenty of free time on my hands while waiting to fly out of country and I didn't choose to fill the empty hours with quality activities. I fell back into drinking, only this time my drinking occurred on the weekdays as well. I avoided multi-day binges at least, as that would be most unwise considering that I could be called into the office at any moment to fly out. During the day time, I worked out heavily at the gym, essentially trying to burn off the effects of the alcohol from the night before. Nights were my own, however, and there wasn't a single night where I didn't have at least ten drinks.

As my drinking wore on that June and July, I could actually feel my health deteriorating. The years of drinking had begun to catch up with me and I found it difficult to perform the physical exercises that used to come so easily to me. My endurance disappeared and my strength waned. A couple years prior, I could run five miles without breaking much of a sweat. That summer, I was hard pressed to run the length of a football field without having to stop and gasp for air.

I kept up my pattern of drinking each night and then recovering in the gym. After six weeks, my clearance finally came through and I was given a flight to Afghanistan. If my security clearance had taken any longer, I don't know what would have become of me. I couldn't seem to put the bottle down no matter how hard I tried.

I finally flew out to Afghanistan on August 12, 2010, and not a moment too soon. As soon as I touched down in Kabul, all thoughts of drinking disappeared. I didn't miss it at all. During my first month overseas, I came to understand a very curious thing. I was only tempted when alcohol was readily available. When alcohol wasn't available, I didn't crave it or think about it.

My yearlong assignment was located in Kabul, the capital of Afghanistan, at the New Kabul Compound, or NKC, for short. Unlike other provinces that had large coalition military bases like Kandahar air base in Kandahar Province, or Camp Leatherneck in the southern province of Helmand, or Mazar-Sharief to the north, Kabul had eleven different compounds of varying sizes located all throughout the city and the surrounding areas.

Bagram air field, or BAF, was located just 20 miles to the north of Kabul. There was also a compound at the airport, another at the embassy, and the compounds of NKC, Camp Phoenix, Blackhorse, Camp Eggers, ISAF, and several other smaller ones in the area surrounding Kabul. Each compound varied in the physical size and number of troops. Camp Phoenix was very large and had thousands of troops. NKC, where I was located, was one kilometer square in size and had roughly 2,000 troops living there. Needless to say, space was tight.

I settled into my new role and responsibilities. I worked for a high-profile task force that managed a program of all the local national security guards. I found the work to be easy, yet interesting, and I threw myself into my assignment whole-heartedly. The work was more administrative in nature than my other deployments. I was also serving at a higher rank, so the operational tempo was slower than my two previous deployments where I was leading and running missions every day, taking enemy fire, and traveling constantly between bases to check out supply routes. Even though the adventure was not there, since I was serving on a joint task force, I interacted at strategic levels with U.S. service members representing the other military branches as well as military personnel from other countries. It was all interesting work.

Now that I was overseas, I had all the time in the world and no distraction in alcohol. I began to attend weekly church services on the base and became close friends with the base chaplain. He and I had many conversations together about life, my drinking, where I was going, and what God was trying to teach me through all of it. As we talked, I came to understand that God had been calling my name for years, only I wasn't seeking Him in return.

The chaplain made things click for me. Suddenly, my struggles and God's apparent lack of response all made perfect sense. I hadn't been doing my part to seek the Lord and turn over my life to His leading. No wonder I had gotten myself into such a mess. I mentally kicked myself for not having discovered that truth sooner. To be sure, I had prayed over and over again for deliverance or forgiveness, but I had never been ready to turn from my sin and follow God. The chaplain told me that deliverance was a two-way street. God would always do His part, but I had to do mine.

Without the constant presence of alcohol, I found it easy to think about God and to spend time reading the Bible and drawing closer to Him. I asked my chaplain friend what I should do when I returned from the deployment, so that I would not lose momentum. His advice was to not forget what I had learned and to not be careless. He told me that sin was constantly out to get me and if I let my guard down, even for an instant, it would take me back and destroy me. After having lived the way that I had for the previous ten years, I completely agreed with him.

Towards the middle of the fall, I approached my chaplain and asked him if he would baptize me. I remember him smiling at me and saying that he had never baptized anyone before and that he would be honored to do so. So, the next Sunday after services, I stood outside of the chapel in my uniform and addressed the congregation that had gathered. I gave them a shortened version of my life, my drinking, and how I believed that the Lord had given me a second chance at life with this deployment. I said that I wanted to make a public declaration of faith. Then I sat down in a kiddie pool full of water and was baptized in the name of the Father, the Son, and the Holy Spirit.

As I came up from the water I felt an incredible sense of peace flood my soul and as I closed my eyes against the sunlight, I could absolutely see an image of Jesus Christ in my mind. It was a beautiful moment, and for the rest of the year during the deployment, I grew closer to the Lord.

13

Following my baptism in the fall of 2010, I continued to pursue my relationship with God while on deployment. I read my Bible nearly every day, and I attended church services in the chapel on the compound at least once, sometimes twice a week. The chapel building itself wasn't much; just a large, rectangular tent with a pulpit and some musical instruments, but it was wonderful all the same.

As 2010 turned into 2011, my role in Afghanistan changed and I took on increased responsibilities. These new duties required me to travel around the country to various bases and give briefings to high ranking officers. Once again, I got busy with my new duties and began to get careless in my walk with Christ. I still attended church services on Sundays, but if I was traveling, I didn't seek out a base chapel and I began to read my Bible less and less.

Looking back, I believed that my amazing experience with God in the fall and my subsequent baptism had freed me from the ravages of my past. While it is true that I was forgiven and redeemed, I hadn't been tested yet outside of the deployment environment. And I still didn't understand that my walk with the Lord was a two-way street. God was always there, waiting to meet with me and talk with me, but if I didn't show up or pour energy into the relationship, things with Him would flounder. My relationship with God was the only thing helping me in my battle against addiction, but I didn't fully grasp that I could eventually be back in the miserable place where I started if I fell away from God again. Still, even though I had lost some of my initial spiritual fervor, I was doing much better overall in terms of my spiritual walk.

The upward momentum was short-lived, however. As my yearlong deployment drew to a close, my career took a severe hit. During deployments, certain Marine Corps regulations and fitness standards are typically relaxed given the stressful environment. In this case, only two months away from the end of my deployment, several senior ranking officers took offense to the fitness regulations that I was not meeting and I received negative marks in my officer's file.

I was thoroughly crushed. The fitness standards were rarely enforced during deployments, but now, due to the technicality, the adverse fitness report would follow me for the rest of my Marine Corps career. There was no way to argue or appeal the rating. The worst thing was that the possibility of promotion to the next rank would now be in question due to the negative rating. The Marines had been my sole identity for nearly nine years, so it was a devastating blow.

I felt that I had given the Marines everything and this was my reward. I was upset at myself for relaxing on the fitness standards while on the deployment, to now find myself in this position. But more so, I was angry that the Marine Corps would allow it to take place. I put on a good show for my superiors for the remaining two months of the deployment, but inside I was furious. For a time, I simply stopped caring about being a Marine officer. I figured that if the Marine Corps was going to treat me this way after nearly a decade of steadfast loyalty and service, then I was through with striving so hard to uphold the dignity of my uniform.

Since the rank of Major in my active duty career was not assured any longer, I started considering the possibility of transitioning to civilian employment. Serving in the Marine Corps in a Reserves capacity would be a viable option during civilian employment, and I was fairly certain of promotion to the rank of Major and higher in the Reserves. But my heart wasn't into the possibilities just yet. The shock to my active duty career was too great.

I spent the last two months of my deployment consumed with the upcoming transition back to the United States and trying to figure out what I would do when I returned home. I would still be joined to my parent command at Headquarters Marine Corps, but I needed to search for housing. After searching online for several weeks, I settled on a condo just south of Washington D.C.

The location of new condo was perfect, about halfway between the Pentagon and Marine Corps Base Quantico. There were shops and stores nearby and a nice gym located a mile or so away. The location was also strategic to defense-related work, so it would be the perfect place to begin looking for civilian employment if I chose to leave the Marine Corps.

~

I FLEW OUT OF KABUL, AFGHANISTAN, ON AUGUST 12, 2011. My first stop was Kuwait and I spent nearly a week there waiting for a flight back to the United States.

Ali Al Salem in Kuwait was a very large U.S. staging base and a thoroughfare for military personnel entering and leaving the Iraq and Afghan theaters. I spent the week in Kuwait going to the gym, sleeping in, and reading in the coffee shops on base. It was a relaxing and peaceful time, in spite of the turmoil of my thoughts. The down time gave me an opportunity to reflect on what I was going to do with my life once I returned home.

Because I had somewhat turned my back on the Marine Corps, I subconsciously decided that my relationship with the Lord could go on the back burner as well. God had been so good to me over the past year, but the bitterness I felt over my active duty Marine Corps career caused me to stop maintaining my relationship with Him. I stopped reading the Bible, praying, attending church, or fellowshipping with other believers. As I withdrew from the Lord, thoughts of alcohol and vice began to resurface in my mind.

My short rest in Kuwait ended and I boarded a commercial flight that took me home to the United States. I flew from Kuwait to Budapest, Hungary, and from there to Shannon, Ireland. I changed planes and flew directly to Washington D.C., then changed planes again and landed in North Carolina at the local airport in Jacksonville. I needed to go onto the base the next morning to check in with my deployed command.

I had arranged for a friend to pick me up from the airport and take me to a hotel where I could spend the night. I checked in with my command the very next day and was given forty-eight hours to report back to my parent command at Headquarters Marine Corps at the Pentagon. So I said goodbye to my friend, drove the five hours north to D.C., checked into my unit, and then checked back out on leave for several days. Then I drove the twenty miles south to my brother's apartment.

My brother and I went to dinner that evening, and I drank again for the first time in almost a whole year. My tolerance to alcohol had greatly diminished during the previous year, and after six or seven drinks, I was well on my way to being drunk. I finally went to sleep around 1 a.m. in my brother's guest room. I woke up the next morning with a raging hangover, but I got myself cleaned up so that we could pick up a rental truck, get my belongings out of storage, and move them into my new place.

Over the next few days, I immersed myself in the task of unpacking. I would turn on the TV or put a movie on for background noise, crack open some beers, and busy myself with putting my condo together. My request for post-deployment leave had been granted and I was looking at the next three weeks off work. There was no compelling interest to stay sober. I was content to drink, stay up late or even pull an all-nighter, unpack, and watch TV. I was wasted every night. It was a repeat of the benders during the spring of 2010, when I started drinking heavily after losing Amy. There was a 7-11 store just three blocks away, so when I ran out of alcohol, I simply waltzed down to the store and restocked.

Over the month that followed, my tolerance for alcohol increased. I found that I needed more and more alcohol to get that feeling that I felt I deserved after all I'd been through. Experienced substance abusers call it the "chaser buzz." A twelve-pack of beer became a fifth of scotch plus a six-pack. When that wasn't sufficient to get the job done, I stepped it up to a fifth and a twelve-pack, or maybe a twenty-four pack of beer and a pint of liquor. Since I wasn't going into the office during those days off work, my routine was soon established around alcohol.

After my morning workout and taking care of any errands that needed to be done, I would start drinking as I accomplished things around my house, whether it was cleaning, organizing, or cooking. I wasn't very particular in what I drank. I didn't care about mixing different kinds of alcohol at all. I drank whatever I had and then walked down to the store to get more. If it was later in the evening, I made sure that I bought enough to get me through the night and into the next day.

After my post-deployment leave ended and it was time for me to go back to work, I faced a new challenge. It felt like I was simply going through the motions of being a Marine. I had become quite jaded. My work wasn't challenging or interesting enough to keep me engaged, and I dreaded having to be there day after day. In hindsight, those feelings only drove me to desire the weekend and drinking that much more. The weekend was my escape from the drudgery and emptiness of the work week.

My weekend routine was the same as before: leave work, stock up on alcohol, drive to the gym and workout, head home, and then crack that first drink and not stop until Sunday afternoon. And the only reason I had to stop on Sundays was because I needed to avoid looking like I had been living in the gutter when I walked into the office on Monday morning.

After each drunken weekend, I felt absolutely awful. My body retained the residual alcohol like a sponge retains water. I was sober, but the dehydration, the shortness of breath, and uncontrollable sweating were enough to make me ill. Each Monday morning, I would swear to myself that the previous weekend was the *last* weekend I would drink like that. But every weekend would be a repeat.

As my health began to deteriorate, my weight increased. I had come back from Afghanistan in August at 6'4", 250 pounds, and very lean and muscular. By November, I was up to around 295 pounds with the 300-pound mark just around the corner. I was smoking cigarettes in addition to drinking. As I continued to drink hardcore, the feelings of shame and guilt came right along with it, the same as every time before. I knew that I was sinning and hurting God with my actions, and I was also hurting my body, but I didn't care any longer about trying to stop.

TO PROVIDE SOME DISTRACTION, I STARTED TO REACH BACK out to girls online. In my current state, I didn't even try to go down the road again with Amy. I needed to get myself together, and to be honest, she knew too much about the worst of me. I wanted a fresh start, and I thought that maybe this was my chance to make up for the hurt and pain that I had caused, by trying to do better this time around.

I had been home for a little over a month when I met a girl online named Heather. She was a strong Christian and a pediatric nurse, and after several dates, we decided to date exclusively and build a relationship together. I was able to keep my drinking a secret from Heather at first. Attending church together helped me not to drink on Saturday nights because I needed to meet her for services on Sunday mornings. I continued to drink every Friday night, however, and any other chance that came around.

The month of September finished out and most of October passed by without any major incidents. Towards the end of October, I had a few days off work and per my usual routine, I fully stocked up on alcohol on that first day by myself. That evening, Heather and I were talking on the phone. We were discussing our relationship and how we felt that the Lord had brought us together, and we were tentatively making future plans.

To my embarrassment, I was drunk by that point, but I still had command over my voice and Heather couldn't hear the alcohol. Because my inhibitions were lowered and I was feeling heightened emotions, I told her that I loved her. As soon as I said the words, I regretted them because I knew they were not true. I liked Heather, liked her a lot. But I didn't love her. It was the alcohol talking, not me. She got quiet for a moment and then rather excitedly told me that she loved me also.

Well, I had put it out there and she took me up on the sentiment, and now I had to run with the professed emotions. I couldn't come back to her and tell her that I had been drinking when I said that I loved her, and that it wasn't quite true. I was sorrowful to know what I had done, and I was upset because alcohol had caused me to start something that I couldn't finish. Even if I did fall in love with her, I knew that she would never marry a drunk like me. I had given her a false hope and it would break her heart when the relationship inevitably ended poorly. What alternative was there? I was drinking heavily and once she found out, I knew she would not stand for a drunk boyfriend, let alone a drunk husband.

October turned into November, and in spite of my efforts to conceal my habit, Heather learned about my drinking. One Saturday afternoon she unexpectedly came over to my house while I was quite drunk. I tried to keep it together as best as I could while she visited, but my secret was out. She stayed for a while, had a drink herself, and then left in the early evening.

The next day, I went to Heather's house and apologized and actually came clean about my drinking problem. She listened for a while and then asked if she could pray for me. I was so embarrassed that I couldn't even look at her. She was going to stick with me and pray for me? A loser like me? I couldn't believe it. She told me that she had dated a couple other men with drinking problems in the past and that the relationships had ended poorly, but she felt that there was something special about me and she wanted to see our relationship through. It seemed that she had already made her peace with my drinking, and to her credit, she never got on my case about drinking again.

Heather and I continued our relationship, and I continued to get drunk on the weekends. As Thanksgiving approached, we decided to spend the holiday at my house. Dinner plans included Heather and myself, my brother, plus another friend or two of hers. The night before Thanksgiving, I went to Heather's house for a pre-holiday get together with some of her church friends. There was plenty of wine and beer available, but I didn't drink anything because I knew that I would have to drive home later. Driving while drunk was not something I took chances with any more, but also, I didn't want to risk looking foolish after a few drinks were in me. Not drinking also made me look like a stand-up guy to her friends.

Besides, I had other plans. I was simply itching to get away from everyone and be done with the niceties so that I could drink alone, in peace. Around 10:30 p.m., I made a lame excuse to Heather about having to leave and then I drove straight to a corner store, stocked up on beer, wine, and champagne, and then headed home to truly party. That evening, I cleaned my house, prepared food for the Thanksgiving meal the next day, and watched TV while I pounded drink after drink. I finally passed out around 3 a.m.

The next morning, I woke up late and began to get ready to host the Thanksgiving meal. My company was coming over in the afternoon, and by the time they arrived, I had everything prepped and ready. As far as meals go, we had a great Thanksgiving, but I was completely drunk the entire time.

The others drank a lot on this occasion too. My brother drank that night, and even Heather and her friend drank too much. Heather had to take a nap on my couch in order to sober up enough to make the drive home. I continued to drink while she slept it off for a couple of hours. I told myself that since *everyone* was drinking, I had the license to drink myself, and even get wasted. In fact, after everyone left I noticed that most of my alcohol was gone, so I staggered down to the corner store to restock.

Around this timeframe, I was starting to be afraid of what would become of me. The guilt and shame from my boozing had begun to reach critical mass. It was all I could think about. The feelings just never went away anymore. Before, it would only take a day or two to feel better about myself. But now, the only way to get rid of the shame and self-loathing was to drink it away. My conscience was alive and well, but I was being eaten alive by guilt.

As I reflected on my situation, I realized that walking with the Lord the previous year had awakened my conscience; now, the Holy Spirit would not let me off the hook. The Lord was shouting my name and asking me to come back to Him, but I would not. The realization was both good and bad. Good because I recognized my own sin, but bad because I kept on drinking anyway. I had surrendered myself to my self-imposed fate and accepted the fact that I was just a plain old drunk. Perhaps a steady walk with the Lord was for other people, but it didn't seem to help me much.

The cycle of abuse continued into December. For Christmas, I decided to go home to Ohio to spend the holiday with my mother, and somehow, I kept it together while I was under her roof. Even though I didn't drink, I thought about alcohol constantly and it was hard to enjoy anything else. After the holiday, I remember how incredibly anxious I felt during the eight-hour drive back to Northern Virginia. Alcohol had such a hold on me that I felt powerless to stand up to it any longer.

During the entire drive, I kept promising myself that I would not drink, I would not drink, and I even listened to my pastor's sermons on my iPad as I drove hour after hour, trying to steel my spiritual resolve. Yet, I knew it was only a matter of time before I would have a drink in my hands. I arrived home around 9 p.m. and went right to the store to get alcohol. As soon as I was inside my house, I cracked the first drink and began to unpack and do laundry. By 3 a.m., I had downed three bottles of wine and twenty beers. I passed out asleep shortly afterwards.

A few hours later, I woke up and right away started in on the alcohol that I had not finished the night before. Sometime that afternoon, my mother called me to see if I had made it home alright. She had some knowledge of my drinking, but didn't know the extent. I typically avoided talking to her during drinking episodes so I could protect her from knowing the full truth. This time I answered the phone. I was so wasted that I could barely get a legible word out. Any attempt at a ruse was up. My mother told me that she was ashamed of me and hung up the phone. I just stared at the phone and thought, *Jordan, you have finally reached your low point. Everyone now knows what you are. They should all be ashamed of you.*

The disgust that was always gnawing at the back of my mind now shoved its way front and center. The internal dialogue continued. *Yes,* I answered myself, *you are a shameful excuse for a human being. Things will never change. You will never change. This is what you are. Just accept it.*

I cracked another beer. I hated what I was doing, but I loved it at the same time, and that made me hate myself even more.

14

I drank myself into despondence that fall and winter of 2011. The feelings of self-loathing had been building for years and had intensified since I returned from Afghanistan in August. I felt dirty and unclean and no amount of showering would fix it. The dirt wasn't just physical; it was also emotional and spiritual filth. The best way that I can describe the feeling is like being a dead man walking. I walked the earth with a sense of having been tried and convicted, with a sentence to be carried out at some undisclosed time.

The weight of that impending doom was crushing. I felt like a condemned man on death row, just waiting for the final appeal to run out and to eventually stare death in the face as I stepped out on that last lonely walk. In fact, when I saw a television program that featured police or prison or death row, my heart kicked and I broke out in a cold sweat.

My self-loathing was so intense that my physical posture changed. I had a hard time looking people in the eye, even if they didn't know my secret. My eyes began to have a haunted look about them. If a friend called and wanted to play golf on a Saturday, I made up some excuse as to why I couldn't play. He knew the real reason I couldn't play was because I would be drunk. And what was worse, I knew that he knew. But we acted like nothing was wrong and went about our weekends. I'd cross paths with him at the office and hang my head in shame because he knew. He *knew*. Here I was, a grown man who was well-educated and had survived three tours in combat, but somehow, I lacked the self-control needed to stay sober long enough to play nine holes of golf. The looks of pity or sympathy made me want to crawl into a hole and vanish.

Drinking caused my voice to lose its confident baritone and instead become sluggish and timid. The voice of the Marine Captain who had commanded men under fire in Iraq and given orders in Afghanistan with confidence and adrenaline was gone. Instead, a broken, haggard voice remained with tones of regret and misery. I remember having to really concentrate on forming the words that I needed in an attempt to speak coherently. Because I was always exhausted and detoxing, my stutter was severely aggravated, and it was nearly impossible to speak a fluid sentence. I couldn't think straight and always found myself in a mental fog.

By the New Year, I noticed a rapid decline in my health. My body was constantly overloaded with residual alcohol and I always felt sick. Because a typical bender was three to four days for me, I was smoking several packs of cigarettes and drinking enough alcohol for ten grown men during each one.

When I got up in the mornings, my entire body ached. My lungs hurt with every breath I took. I was severely dehydrated, but rather than drink water, I kept drinking more and more alcohol. As a result, my blood became thick and sluggish and my heart had to work overtime to pump it through my system. Over time, this wore me down to the point of exhaustion. My endurance was shot. I'd try to walk up a flight of stairs and have to stop half way up to catch my breath. While sitting at my computer or driving somewhere, I would suddenly break out in cold sweats for no reason. I also experienced a loss of motor control. Lying in bed, my limbs would randomly twitch and I had to concentrate intently to perform the simplest of tasks.

One of the worst symptoms that I experienced was memory loss. I consumed so much alcohol that it wiped my memory clean so many times, and there are portions of my life that I simply cannot remember. I try to recall memories or events that supposedly happened while I was drinking and I cannot do it. In fact, during the fall of 2011, I had several four to five-day benders where I blacked out and lost whole days at a time.

One of these mini vacations from work started on a Wednesday and ended Monday morning. At the end of the period, my brother text messaged me asking what I had been up to all week. I responded, "What do you mean *all week*? It's only Friday." I was shocked to realize it was Monday. Somewhere in there, I had lost track of three days, and I have absolutely no memory of them to this day.

When I was on those three to five-day binges, I was afraid to check my cell phone for text messages, emails, or missed calls. I dreaded sobering up and reading the aftermath of conversations that I participated in while drunk. Sometimes, my phone was clear and I breathed a sigh of relief. Other times, I was horrified and humiliated by what I read. I got to the point of hiding my cell phone in another part of my apartment so that I would not be tempted to drunkenly text people or write flippant emails. I figured that if I couldn't control myself, then I would just hide my cell phone, as a preemptive move. Sometimes it worked and sometimes it didn't.

Heather stuck with me through December and most of January, but I had already cooled towards her. Even though she denied it, my drinking was finally getting under her skin. She began to treat me differently, like someone to be tolerated or pitied and not taken seriously. That made me want to be with her even less and I just couldn't keep up the game with her anymore. I ended our relationship in the middle of January.

In the midst of what I was putting myself through, I still longed for companionship, especially when I was between girlfriends. Whenever I was lonely, I went back to my habit of meeting women online on social sites, striking up conversations, and going out with them. This always involved alcohol. Being drunk afforded me the opportunity to say things to women that I would never have the courage or the conscience to say while sober. Some of the dates were with Christian women of character, but most were not. During the low periods of my life, but also the high periods, I used alcohol to give myself a needed ego boost by attracting women and getting high off their attention.

These short-term dating relationships never went far; one or both used each other for our own purposes and then moved on when that purpose was fulfilled. We would find someone else to pursue or we just stopped caring about each other. But my drinking was certainly a huge reason that these relationships never worked out. I simply wasn't capable of putting a woman's needs before my own.

Waking up hungover, I would see messages on my phone from girls telling me to get lost. I knew that the rejection from women wasn't because of my looks or professional status. Instead, drinking was so ingrained in me that women couldn't compete with alcohol's place in my life. It actually felt like I was cheating on alcohol by going on a date with a woman, and in the end, the bottle always won.

THE PHYSICAL CONSEQUENCES OF DRINKING WERE HARD, BUT one afternoon I also realized the monetary cost of my alcohol abuse through the years. I was sitting at my desk, reflecting over the mess I had made of things. It was payday and I had just checked my bank account. I was startled by all of the liquor and beer transactions. For the first time, I took a calculator and did some figuring.

I went back in time to The Basic School and all those months of going out to bars and clubs in the Washington D.C. area. During the prime evening hours, I decided that the average liquor drink was approximately $10.00 and the average pint of beer was around $7.00. Given those numbers, and given the number of drinks I consumed on an average weekend of going to bars and clubs in those days, the dollar cost totaled around $200.00 per weekend. In later years, once I decided to do the predominance of my drinking at home, I concluded that the dollar amount that I spent on alcohol was approximately the same, because I was getting more alcohol for my money. Frequently, I bought cases of foreign beer and $60 bottles of scotch, so $200 per weekend was still a reasonable average.

As I continued calculating that afternoon, I realized that if I had spent $200 for most weekends over the last fourteen years, then I had spent more than $100,000 on alcohol. I was appalled. Over the years, I had wondered how much money was spent getting drunk, but I had never put it all together and totaled it up like this. I could have saved that money for a house. I could have paid for a graduate degree or traveled the world over. I could have invested the money or used it to help my family or others in need. Instead, I chose to spend the money getting wasted over and over again. God had blessed me, and instead, I had squandered those resources.

ON THE SURFACE, LIFE KEPT GOING. MOST PEOPLE THOUGHT I was a normal, standup guy, and that everything was fine. But it was a carefully crafted facade. Alcohol had made me a master of deceit. If I wanted to keep drinking and still maintain some sort of dignity in the eyes of others, I had no other choice but to lie. Allowing people to see the real me would be too devastating.

So, I became very good at crafting cover stories and deceiving the people around me. Living a double life might sound fun and glamorous, but it is exhausting work, and unsustainable the longer it goes on. I liken it to having multiple identities, all competing for time and space within your mind. I had to keep track of multiple behavior patterns, histories, and likes/dislikes, all matched up with different people. It was a challenge to keep everything coherent and the stories straight, and be able to recall them at a moment's notice in case I needed to give an answer for something.

I found that the easiest lies to tell were the ones that were 90% true. The fewer details that I had to lie about, the fewer stories I had to keep straight in my own head. I had to make sure that my cover stories fit with my personality and behavior patterns. If I told someone an outlandish cover story, they would see through it in an instant. When I first began drinking, making up stories about my whereabouts or people that I had been with was easy. As a college student, drinking was expected, so I didn't have many occasions where I needed to lie, except to assuage any worries from my parents.

Later on in the Marine Corps, drinking was also an expected part of relaxing on the weekend, so I didn't have the need to create many cover stories there either. It wasn't until I first moved to Washington D.C. and began to build a life in addition to the Marine Corps that I needed to become exceptionally good at living a double life. I was balancing a work life, a romantic life, a church life, and a family life, and I found myself creating multiple versions of myself for each one.

During the week I went to my office, the gym, kept in contact with my family, and swapped emails with friends. On the weekends, I was drinking. In order to not get caught, I pulled out one of my cover stories as to why I was unavailable for recreation or dates or even for family. For example, my mother would call me on Sunday evenings and ask if I had been to church that morning and whether I enjoyed the message. Often, I had not gone to church because I was royally drunk. But I couldn't admit that to my mom, so I would be sure to go to the church's website and download the sermon notes. Then when she called, I would be able to tell her what the sermon was about, as well as craft who I had seen at church, or what was going on in my Bible study.

When my relationship with Amy first started, I was in a short period of sobriety, so I didn't need to create excuses for her at first. Then I started adding the alcohol back in, so if I wanted to drink on a weekend, I had to craft a story about spending time with family or helping out a friend with something. The lying kept my drinking hidden from her for a while, but of course she eventually found out during the major incidents in our relationship. Later when we were on the rocks, Amy would text me on Saturdays and ask if I was sober. Of course, I told her that I was, but I wasn't. I even sent her pictures from golf courses to prove to her that I wasn't holed up at home drinking. I had snapped many pictures at various golf courses with my cell phone and I would send one of the saved pictures back to her via text. I don't know whether she believed me every time or not, but I had to keep up the impression that I was staying away from the bottle.

After the break up with Amy and during my several-month binge, I had to become even better at lying, but my skills started to wear out. It was becoming too much. I made mistakes and people began to see through the facade. I told one family member one story and then told another family member another story, not realizing that they had already compared notes. Then I was busted. Later on, after I got back from Afghanistan the second time and got heavily back into drinking, I made excuses to Heather while we were dating or skipped out on social activities so I could get home to drink alone.

After Heather and I broke up, there were periods that I was dating several girls at the same time and throwing alcohol into the mix, and I had to remember which lies I had told to which girl in which instance. After a time, I could no longer keep things straight and they also called me out.

The truly sad thing is that lying and being deceitful had become just par for the course. They had become *part* of me. I had practically no conscience about it. Lying was simply what was required to maintain my way of life. Whenever lies caught up with me, I did feel some measure of regret. Not regret for having lied or sinned, but regret that I had been caught, that I had potentially hurt someone, and that the relationship would now have to change or end.

One of the worst consequences of my drinking was the constant state of fear in which I lived. As ironic as it sounds, I came to be afraid to be around alcohol. I began to fear the effects it had on me, what it made me say and do. I don't mean fear in the physical sense, like being afraid of heights, or public speaking, or closed-in spaces. Those are natural fears that can more easily be overcome. Rather, the fear that I experienced was deeper, more psychological, more controlling, and more damaging.

I was afraid that if I were on a date and a woman ordered wine with the meal, that it would trigger an uncontrollable reaction in me to sabotage the date just to head to a store and purchase my own bottle for later. If I was at a social gathering and the guys were drinking beer, I was afraid that I would drink far too much and embarrass myself beyond the point of humor. Since I cringed at the idea of being subject to people's pity or ridicule, I ended up not going to places because it was better to avoid the situation, and the possibility of embarrassment, entirely. That's how much alcohol was dictating my life.

I was also afraid of professional loss. I had decided to start interviewing for civilian jobs, but I still had a few months left to go on active duty. I was afraid that prospective employers would see through my professional persona and realize that I was just a drunk and refuse to hire me. But more than all of those worries combined, I became afraid of spending time alone with myself, because I knew that I would end up drinking away all of my free time and wasting all of my potential.

I had tried to stop drinking so many times, with each attempt ending in failure. For a time, I would fill up my weekend schedule with events to prevent myself from drinking —dates, church activities, social outings, family get-togethers, golf outings. I discovered that if I truly kept my schedule busy enough, I could abstain from alcohol for a weekend or two. But then I ended up resenting the distractions and cutting out early to get home and drink.

Since my duty to the Marine Corps was the only thing grounding me sometimes, I would use the motivation of my job to try to curb my drinking. I would stay late at the office to get more accomplished and would even use sleep as an alcohol deterrent. After working late at the office, I would come home and right away take a nap until 10 pm to keep myself from drinking. Then I would get up, head to the gym, and workout until after midnight when I could no longer buy alcohol. This strategy worked until I found myself skipping the gym in order to drink. Since the gym was necessary to stay in shape for the Marine Corps, pushing my gym time until late at night quickly became unsustainable. Instead, after coming home from the gym, I resorted to taking several doses of sleep medication to knock myself out so that I would fall asleep and not drink. Again, the strategy worked for a time but alcohol always found me.

Through the years, I had tried many, many things. I had enrolled in graduate courses on the weekends to give myself a worthwhile pursuit to fill up my free time. I had tried going to Alcoholics Anonymous meetings. I had tried looking for accountability from my men's Bible study group. And I had certainly tried all kinds of ways to moderate my drinking and step it down gradually. Rather than two bottles of wine and eighteen beers, for example, I would determine that a single bottle of wine and a six-pack would be it for me. The only problem with that strategy was that I went through it too fast and there was too much night left at the end of the alcohol. Just like a junkie needing a fix, I would have a desperate need to score more. Moderation was impossible. And the 7-11 store was just around the corner.

I tried anything and everything if it would keep me from drinking. For a while, some of these strategies worked. But there was no lasting relief, just a temporary distraction. I put my hope in these strategies as a kind of bullet proof vest or magic talisman that would protect me from myself. But it would only take one stumble, just one time where my defenses didn't work and I ended up drunk and the magic of that strategy would be gone. Then I would be right back where I started.

I had come to a point in my life where one more step in the direction I was headed might mean physical death. Throughout the week, I would think about my next binge and wonder if it would be my final one… if I would finally drink too much alcohol and float away to the afterlife. It seemed inevitable; I had abused alcohol for so long that I was convinced I had done irreparable damage to my heart and liver. I prayed, but I figured that I had blown all of my chances with God and He wasn't listening any more. I began thinking about just accepting my fate and letting the chips fall where they may, but I was terrified.

I reached the place of admitting that I was powerless over alcohol. Once upon a time, I was the one to hold the bottle and it served the purposes I had in mind. But as the years went by, I slowly became a slave to alcohol, and alcohol now had me by the throat. I feared that I would be its slave for the rest of my life and that it would never let me go. My greatest fear was that of dying, either by alcohol or by my own hand. I thought about dying all the time; death always seemed to be lurking just out of sight. Only while in the midst of drinking did the *fear* of death and suicide seem to vanish, but I still thought about dying constantly.

The scariest part of coming off a binge was the suicidal mind play that happened at night. My sleep was always restless. I tossed and turned all night long, never being able to get comfortable or stop my heart from racing. As l laid in bed with my eyes closed, my mind envisioned thoughts of death. I saw myself sitting at my dining room table, a bottle of scotch beside me, writing a suicide note that told the world how hopeless my life had become and that I would be doing the world a favor by leaving it. Then, I would see myself pick up one of my handguns, place the barrel against my temple and pull the trigger, only to tumble down a dark and turbulent tunnel towards the waiting gates of hell. At that moment, my eyes would snap open and I would sit up in bed gasping for air. Words cannot express how terrifying it was to watch myself take my own life and have my mind vividly fill in all the horrible details.

After several weeks of fitful, suicidal dreams, I locked my handguns away in a closet just in case I actually tried to kill myself while intoxicated. I knew of a few people in college that had done just that. They were in rehab for alcoholism and when faced with having to turn their backs on alcohol or get clean, they chose to leave treatment behind and take their own lives instead. The visions and memories scared me so badly that I cried out to God to please take them away. I was scared to die, but I didn't want to live either, at least not as I had been living.

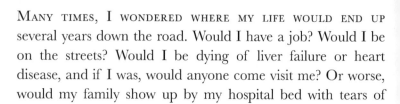

Many times, I wondered where my life would end up several years down the road. Would I have a job? Would I be on the streets? Would I be dying of liver failure or heart disease, and if I was, would anyone come visit me? Or worse, would my family show up by my hospital bed with tears of regret, sadness, and pity? I don't think I could have handled that.

Yet, at the same time, a life without alcohol seemed overwhelming to me, as desperately as I wanted that. Alcohol had been a part of my life for so long that the thought of giving it up left me empty inside. Having to face life without my favorite companion seemed unbearable. I wasn't sure that I wanted to go on living if I had to face life alone.

Sometimes my despairing thoughts made me feel like no one in the universe cared if I lived or if I died. Of course, my immediate family cared, but I was estranged from them on an intimate level. My middle brother knew my secret, but he didn't have the power to help me. And he truly didn't know how bad it was, the depths to which I had fallen, or the hopelessness of my thoughts.

My mother also knew I drank and expressed displeasure and hurt over my drinking habits; still, she didn't fully grasp the seriousness of my plight. I shielded her from knowing how badly I was doing because I didn't want to cause her more angst. Even though she never would have turned her back on me, I just couldn't bring myself to let her know the full truth. The idea of bringing her that level of disappointment and sadness was something I couldn't bear.

My father and my youngest brother had no idea how bad my drinking was and I made sure to keep it that way. Friends were either in the dark or didn't know how to help, and I kept them at a distance. Sure, I'd talk, email, and text with everyone, but only superficially. There wasn't any real depth or substance to our conversations. I certainly didn't want to tell anyone how much of a drunk I'd become, or how I was losing hope.

So, I'd wake up in the morning and consider the day ahead and feel complete blackness and void before me; not one thing to look forward to, not one person to fully know me. No one to *really* talk to. I went through the motions, but I felt disconnected from everyone and everything. My life was so wrought with sin that I didn't know the way back to God this time, even though I had walked with Him before. The only seeming answer was another drunken binge to dull the pain. I felt like a hollow shell without a soul, no substance, no nothing. On certain days, the feelings were so lonely, so torturous, and so all-consuming, that I wondered if I even cast a shadow as I walked the earth. Other days I would sit on my couch and watch television and just cry; even fictional characters on television had more hope than I did.

Thoughts of my death continued to follow me. I wondered how I would die. Would it be from alcohol poisoning? I had certainly consumed enough. Would I die from suicide? I had plenty of weapons and anti-depressant medication. Most pressing, if I did leave this earth, would I wake up in heaven where I would finally be at peace? Or would I wake up in hell because I had never truly experienced the saving power of Jesus Christ? I was so lost and confused that I didn't know any more.

One night I dreamt of dying and then waking up in a white amphitheater, with God sitting at one end and me standing at the other. Waterfalls of brilliant light cascaded from His presence as lightning and thunder exploded from His throne. Angels filled the stadium as stars raced by through the blackness of outer space. God asked His angels to find my name in the Book of Life. There was so much power in His voice that the very universe shook. In my dream, I envisioned God in His utter, brilliant majesty leveling His finger at me from afar and telling me that I was a loser and that He would never let me enter heaven. Oh yes, eternal punishment would be my fate, my tortured imaginings seemed to say. The marble floor beneath my feet broke and crumbled as God proclaimed my fate, and I fell down to the waiting gates of hell.

As a child I had prayed the sinner's prayer to ask Jesus Christ into my heart and life, but now as an adult, where were the repentant actions in my life that showed I was serious about my faith? Where was the changed life that demonstrated true transformation from the inside out, the proof of living for Christ? Those behaviors were not present in my life, if they ever had been. I questioned whether I was saved and had merely fallen away, or whether I had ever been a true Christian.

I had grown up in the church, but I was lukewarm to all of the teaching. Was I truly a believer? Did I possess merely head knowledge about Jesus Christ and what faith meant, but no heart knowledge? I truly didn't know where I stood, or how God viewed me. My sinful actions seemed to belie my claim of salvation. I knew what awaited non-believers after their physical death and I was fearful that I was headed there on a first-class ticket.

As I pondered all of these things, I became more and more depressed and sank into a deep melancholy. I was full of regret. Regret for my choices and how they had led me to this point. Regret for lying to my family and the few friends that cared about me. Regret for how I had treated women over the years, some of whom had truly loved me and tried to help. And regret for myself, because I seemed to be out of options and it was all my own fault.

Life had become dull and empty. Dark thoughts plagued me. *Why go on living? Why keep trying to eke out such a miserable existence?* I tried to shake myself out of my depressed stupor. Had I really reached a point in life where I was contemplating taking my own life?

I felt like I was beyond repair. I had lived a sinful life for too many years. I had hurt myself and I had hurt too many people that cared about me. I was a drunk and nothing about me was redeemable. The feelings of self-loathing only made my drinking all the more intense. The only escape from my misery was to drink and drink until the feelings were gone.

Alcohol was a wonderful mask that made me forget my pain. But I knew that when I sobered up, the tortured feelings would return and I would have to face the person in the mirror again.

15

By January 2012, I was seriously looking for a way out. The disgust I felt towards myself was overwhelming. This was not a new concept for me. I had been self-conditioned to beat myself up for years, and a lot had pushed me to this place.

That winter, I sat in my apartment night after night, and thought about my life and how I had gotten to where I was. After a time, a single word kept rising to the surface of my thoughts. *Brokenness.* Was I damaged goods? I certainly felt like it. For most of my childhood and young adult years I had lived with the conclusion that I wasn't like other people. I was shy and introverted. I couldn't speak easily. I had a hard time striking up conversations and fitting in with people. Meaningful relationships with women seemed elusive. It seemed like everyone else was playing the game of life with a royal flush and all I could scrape together was a pair of lousy twos.

Now so many years removed, I began to take a real, hard inventory of my life for the first time. My parents divorced when I was young. I was raised in a split home, shy and socially awkward, and my speech impediment affected every aspect of my life. My hobbies and interests didn't fit the mold, and furthermore, my desire to fit in and overcome personal struggles had driven me to make poor life choices. I experienced rejection by many of my peers, topped by romantic failures. Even though I accomplished professional and academic feats in spite of my personal struggles, I compartmentalized the successes away from my identity and all I could see was the negative. The truth was that I didn't like who I was on the inside, and I had been self-medicating with alcohol for years.

I'd realized early on that I wasn't like the other children around me. My stutter was the biggest source of shame in my life. Some children are born with a stutter that they eventually outgrow, or they acquire a stutter through physical trauma. In my case, I inherited my stutter from my paternal grandfather. Because my stutter was hereditary, speech therapy could only accomplish so much and it would never disappear completely. I couldn't talk or joke with friends without stuttering, and early on I learned that children can be cruel to one another, so I tended to be quiet and shy.

My stutter notwithstanding, other boys and girls seemed to gravitate towards me during my childhood. Moving to the backwoods of Maine and being homeschooled for a few years gave me a reprieve in terms of my stutter. The isolated setting also set the stage for how my hobbies and interests developed and influenced how I interacted with others. My two younger brothers were my playmates and we became close with a small group of other homeschooling families with like-minded interests. I didn't have to deal with the classroom school environment or any social cliques, and I was free to enjoy pursuits like reading, music, and history.

After moving back to Ohio towards the end of elementary school, it didn't take long to figure out that what I liked and considered normal didn't fit in with city living. Living in Maine was akin to taking a four-year time-out in social development, and it was a rude awakening to return to Ohio. Relocating brought new pressures of trying to fit in and being liked by neighborhood kids. The last thing I wanted to be was "different." But my hobbies, interests, and social patterns had already been formed. I was constantly ridiculed in school. My natural introversion and shyness only intensified the effects of my stutter.

I tried to hide myself in the background and conditioned myself not to speak. I was afraid to read aloud and cringed inside any time that I was forced to do so. If a teacher called on me to answer a question, I played dumb and just didn't answer. After a few seconds, the teacher would move on to someone else. I always knew the answers, but staying quiet was so much safer. Better to be thought of as ignorant rather than kids making fun of me for stuttering.

Instead of pushing myself to interact with my classmates, I withdrew and kept to myself even more. My activities still tended to be solitary endeavors. For example, I played the piano instead of pickup games of basketball. I read books instead of playing sports or video games with friends. I chose to be with my brothers rather than the neighborhood kids. When many of my classmates sat together during lunch, I sat with one or two of my friends who were also on the social fringe. After all, we had something in common; each of us struggled to fit in.

It seemed that everyone had a group except me. The jocks had their group. The cheerleaders had their group. The studious girls and guys each had their group. The musicians had their group. Even the outcasts had formed a group. I had characteristics that belonged in each social group, but I was never totally accepted anywhere. I could dabble with the different groups and spend a little time with each, but full integration and acceptance didn't seem to be in the cards for me.

By the time I finished high school, I had formed a new

social group; me, myself, and I. When I got to college, I began to fit in a little more, but in a different way. I was accepted because I could buy alcohol for minors. I became the go-to guy. Other than that, people didn't care to get to know me as a person. Rather, they wanted to know me in terms of what I could do for them. As my college years went by, I was able to develop a small network of guy friends, but on the romantic scene, I still felt like I was always on the outside looking in.

Throughout my teenage years, I'd had crushes. In fact, I had a new crush each new school year. Sometimes more than one. I would ask girls out, even though I was too nervous to ask them out in person because of my stutter. It sounds silly now, but the adolescent fashion of the day was crafting a nice note, sticking it in the girl's locker and waiting for a response. Sooner or later the girl would get the note and either answer me back with a flat-out *no*, or just put the note in the trash and never respond. This pattern continued throughout high school and it left me feeling unwanted and unlikeable.

By the time I reached my senior year of high school, I had never been on a real date. As my senior year wrapped up and the prom came around, I still didn't have a date for the event. I asked three different girls to go with me and each of them made up some story that she wasn't going to the prom and so she couldn't accept my request. I decided to just go to the prom on my own. And then those same girls showed up at the prom with underclassmen on their arms. I sat through dinner at the prom, dateless, with a painted smile on my face, while inside I was devastated. Even the social outcasts were able to overcome and find each other. I was the only person at the prom without a date. That night seemed to never end. A couple of the other social outcasts would come over from time to time and we would talk, but most of the time I was alone. As the sun came up the next morning and we left the building, I felt rejected and humiliated.

Those kinds of experiences did nothing for my self-esteem.

I can sum up my entire childhood, teenage, and college years with a simple statement: I didn't like myself. In fact, I loathed myself. I didn't think about my life and count my blessings from God. Instead, I could only see the negative experiences that happened to me. I felt sorry for myself and I didn't want to live the rest of my life in the same manner. Something needed to change or happen for me.

The something that entered my life was the Marine Corps. Things began to dramatically change for me once I graduated from boot camp and then completed officer's school. I had earned my place in an elite group of warriors. My physical appearance went through a complete overhaul and my self-confidence soared. I felt real fulfillment for the first time in my life. I could relate to my fellow Marines. We all suffered through the same boot camp and my fellow officers had also been through officer's school like me. We trained together and we went to war together. Those experiences built bonds that transcended normal friendships. Even if I didn't personally know anything about another Marine, we still shared that bond of brotherhood. I finally belonged somewhere.

Active duty service was a great time in my life. Yet it was also at this point that my brokenness manifested itself the strongest. I'd felt like a victim for the majority of my life, so when I became a Marine officer and was invested with power, money, and influence, I decided to make up for lost time and take control of things for the first time. In particular, I didn't need to play defense with women anymore. I was fit, lean, and good-looking, and women began to flock to me. Too often, I turned the hurt of my past onto them and used women for my own gain. I had no interest in real and meaningful relationships during those periods. Since I'd been scorned for so many years, I felt that it was time to turn the tables in a sort of weird style of revenge.

For the first time, I was in control and could do what I wanted and get *who* I wanted. However, there was one caveat in the mix—I was still shy and timid around women. And so, I needed alcohol to give me the courage to begin and end those relationships and to go through with the inevitable hurt that I caused. Had I been sober, I could never have done those things. My first thought upon encountering a pretty woman, honed by so many years of rejection, was that she would never want to get to know me. The next thought would be that with alcohol, all things are possible. So, I'd strike up a conversation, knowing that alcohol would be introduced at some point, and time after time, things would work to my advantage. Since I had been abusing alcohol for several years already, continuing to abuse it in order to have women like me was a natural progression.

Besides abusing my relationships with women, alcohol represented a personal indulgence for myself. Money had always been scarce in my family. Growing up, we didn't have money for vacations, toys, new clothes, lots of gifts, or any of the extras that others seemed to take for granted. My family scrimped and saved every penny. Hand-me-down clothes and thrift store toys were a given.

With that backdrop, whenever an opportunity to indulge myself presented itself, I took it. As a child, this behavior played out when eating out at buffet-style restaurants where there were no limits on how much I could eat. Then once I had my first job when I was 15, I enjoyed having some money of my own for the first time in my life. Rather than saving the money, I spent it on things that I wanted: food, movies, clothes. I found that the enjoyment I got from spending money and indulging myself helped to temporarily dull the pain and struggle from my childhood and teenage years. While this was an immature approach to the world, it made sense to me at the time.

After I turned twenty-one, alcohol became my favorite indulgence to hide my pain. It was perfect. Alcohol wasn't all that expensive, it allowed me to be social and overcome my stutter, it lowered my inhibitions, and it made me feel good. Throughout college and my early years in the Marine Corps, I used alcohol as a tool to boost my confidence, bolster my courage, and help me finally feel like I was on the winning end of things.

Alcohol never stood me up. Alcohol never told me *no*. Alcohol never told me that I was a loser. Alcohol made me feel like I could take on anything. I became increasingly dependent on alcohol to keep me going. Rather than getting better at life or improving myself where I struggled, I self-medicated my problems away. I wasn't mature enough to realize that rather than making my life better, I was only making things worse for myself by leaning on my crutch. The alcohol worked as a mask to keep the truth hidden from myself for a long while.

16

I kept on having severe drinking episodes, one after another, throughout that winter of 2011. I somehow managed to pull myself together and scrape by on New Year's Eve and the early days in January without getting wasted. But one more severe binge towards the middle of January 2012 finally hit me hard enough to make some changes in my life.

My father was going to be flying into town to visit my brother and me for several days. I offered to pick him up at the airport and let him stay at my condo so that he wouldn't have to spend money on a hotel, and he welcomed the opportunity. Leading up to my dad's visit, I had been trying hard to get my drinking habit under control. It was a brand-new year, and amazingly, I hadn't had a drink in two weeks. However, the itchy feeling to get wasted had been building for days.

All during the work week before my dad was set to arrive, I thought about drinking. By the time Friday rolled around, I just couldn't resist any longer and by that evening I was very drunk. I kept telling myself to pull it together because I knew I would have to be sober enough to drive to the airport to pick up my father on Sunday. To no avail. I drank straight through the night and into Saturday morning. When I ran out of alcohol, I staggered down to the corner store and bought more beer and snacks. I pounded drink after drink that entire Saturday until well past midnight and then finally passed out on my couch.

I woke up late on Sunday morning with so much residual alcohol in my system that I was still drunk. My heart began to race as soon as my mind began to clear. I had promised to pick up my father from the airport around 8 p.m. How could I do that if I was still hammered? By 4 p.m. I had sobered up somewhat, but not nearly enough to drive. My brother lived several miles away and I called him and begged him to bail me out. I asked him to pick me up and we could both drive to the airport. He was furious at me for springing it on him so late in the day, but he had pity on my predicament and agreed to help me out. Still, he gave me a tongue lashing most of the way to the airport.

We picked up my father on time and drove back to my place. By the time we arrived home, I was sober enough to drive, and so my father and I went to get a late dinner. Either he had no idea what I had been doing all weekend, or he hid his feelings very well. I'd never been drunk in front of him before, so perhaps he thought my detoxing symptoms were nothing more than me getting over a winter cold.

Our time together that week was good. I was able to leave the office a little earlier than usual, so my dad and I got to spend a lot of time together. Some evenings were spent talking and some were spent watching TV. We even hit quite a few buckets of golf balls. Other than my brother joining us for dinner a couple times, it was just me and my dad. The time flew by. When the following Sunday came around, my brother and I drove my father back to the airport in the afternoon. We said our goodbyes and then we headed back to my house. Despite the severity of my last binge and the week-long sober period that followed, the urge to drink had returned in full force.

The following day was Martin Luther King Jr. Day. Because of the federal holiday, the Marines at my command were given a 72-hour holiday. This vacation period started the previous Friday and I added on a day of personal leave, so I didn't have to report back to work until Wednesday morning. I already knew what I was going to do with my free time. I couldn't deny the insistent voice in my head.

When we got back to my place, my brother got his car and headed home. Immediately, I went to the grocery store to stock up with enough alcohol to get through the next two days. I drove back to my condo with my back seat full of beer and a couple bottles of wine. I cracked the first drink the moment I walked in the door. I drank and watched movies and hung around my condo for two days without sleep. Even though the duration wasn't as long as some of my previous binges, the intensity of this one truly frightened me. To this day, I can't remember half of it. All I remember is always having a drink in my hand, and as soon as I would finish one drink I would immediately get another. When I ran out of alcohol, I staggered down to the store and bought more. I was so wasted and incoherent that I don't know how I was even able to make it there and back to my condo.

Tuesday afternoon arrived and I couldn't absorb one more drop. My body was shutting down and I wondered frantically if I had finally overdone it. Had I finally pushed it too far and this was it for me? I remember getting into bed around 7 p.m. on Tuesday night and passing out, terrified of not waking up again.

I slept until midnight, then tossed and turned until finally falling out of bed just after 6 a.m. on Wednesday morning. I remember feeling hollowed out and totally worthless, but somewhat amazed to be alive. I stumbled into my bathroom to get ready for work. I was detoxing and had to will my hands to stop shaking as they held the razor to my face. It hurt to breathe and my eyes were bloodshot. As I showered and put on my uniform, all I could think about was how I should have died from alcohol poisoning. In two and a half days I had consumed four packs of cigarettes, three bottles of wine, a bottle of champagne, and upwards of fifty beers. I concluded that the only reason I was still alive was my high alcohol tolerance and the mercy of God.

As I drove to the base, my hands continued to shake and I broke out in cold sweats. My heart was under so much pressure that it was racing inside my chest. Somehow, I made it through the main gates on base without causing an accident. I parked in my usual spot and took the elevator to my office; I was in no condition to take the stairs. As soon as I sat down at my desk, people around me could tell that something was wrong. I felt awful, and apparently, I looked it too. My boss actually came over and sat down and asked me if I was ok. I told him that I was fine. I couldn't tell him the truth… that I was a hopeless drunk who just had a brush with death.

ALL DAY LONG I THOUGHT ABOUT MY SITUATION AND FELT wrecked to my soul. Would I even make it through another drunken binge or have another chance to redeem myself? I was scared that I would not survive the next time. Deep down, I knew that the only way out of this misery that I called my life was to totally and completely throw myself at the foot of God's throne and beg Him for mercy. I was desperate for His help, and His way forward. I would accept any punishment, any consequence, just to be free from the scourge of alcohol and the accompanying dejection. This soul-wrenching remorse stayed with me throughout the day until I got home that evening.

That night, I went into my library and fell on the floor and wept and wept and wept. The pent up emotions from the entire day—no, from the past weeks, months, and *years*—all came out in a huge outflowing of remorse and sorrow. I cried so hard that a large dark spot began to form on the Persian rug in the middle of the floor. My body shook with emotion as wave after wave of guilt and shame washed over me. I cried out to God like never before. I had called on the Lord many times in the past, but always on my own terms, like a temporary bandage when things got worse than usual. This time, I was ready to do business with God on His terms. But that meant I had to own up to my sin and confess that I was consciously choosing sin over God when I insisted on doing things my way. I had been my own lord and master for so many years that it was hard to give up my own way, even though I knew I had made a complete mess of things.

As much as I wanted to be my own master, I wanted to be whole and healthy and loved and forgiven by God *more*. So, there on the floor of my library, I came clean to God about everything and asked His forgiveness for my wanton behaviors. I begged God to forgive me and become the Lord and Master of my life and bring some sense of order to the chaos I had created. I needed Him to patch the deep hole in my soul and to replace alcohol with Himself. I needed God in my life day in and day out. My problems were a behavioral outpouring of a spiritual vacuum.

After a time, I picked myself up from the floor of my library and I knew that God had forgiven me. There was no audible voice or ringing bells, but I knew deep in my spirit that I had been forgiven and that I could have true victory over alcohol – *IF* I did it God's way and kept myself in close communion with Him. I realized that walking day-to-day with the Lord was where I always went astray.

The shame and the guilt were still with me, but they were fading. I leaned back against a bookcase and reflected on what had just happened to me, and also what felt different this time.

I thought back to when I got baptized in Afghanistan the year before. I shared a beautiful moment with the Lord after making my public declaration of faith. I had felt forgiven and so strong and at peace. Why hadn't it stuck? At that time, God wasn't really competing with anything in my life. I was deployed to a foreign country where my days were routine and mission-focused. There were no distractions, and alcohol wasn't around. It was easy to focus on God in that environment. This time would be different. I would have to make a conscious choice, with all the temptations fully around me, to turn from drinking and run to God.

I looked across my library and my eyes fell upon my desk. My Bible was laying there. I walked across the room, picked up my Bible, and sat down in an armchair to read. Alcohol had been my god for so long that without it, life seemed bleak and impossible. I knew that I would inevitably fall back into my sinful behaviors unless I replaced alcohol with God's Word.

Reading God's Word. What a simple yet profound thing. In the Bible we are given a glimpse of the majesty, mercy, and mind of God. So to truly know God, we must read about Him and medicate on His Words to us. In addition, the Word of God is a powerful weapon that can beat any addiction, any sin in one's life. Scripture says this about the Bible: *"For the Word of God is living and powerful, and sharper than any two-edged sword, piercing even to the division of soul and spirit, and of joints and marrow, and is a discerner of the thoughts and intents of the heart"* (Hebrews 4:12 NKJV). Reading this passage struck me with wonder that the Word of God can discern my innermost thoughts and intentions. And of course, the reference to weaponry was not lost on my military mind. I realized that I was lacking this kind of power and discernment in my life. I'd been trying to do it all by myself for so many years, but true power comes from being immersed in God's Word.

I spent time reading some of the Apostle Paul's letters in

the New Testament. In Galatians, Paul wrote about having freedom in Christ. In Philippians, Paul wrote about having complete joy in life. In Ephesians, Paul wrote about living by faith and using the Word of God to defend oneself against attacks of the enemy. I read verse after verse about the Holy Spirit and walking by faith. I read verses about living a life of personal holiness. I read verses about how God wants to help us defeat our sinful nature and walk with Him and rely on Him for everything in our lives. Every page that I flipped to and every passage that I perused gave me new spiritual insights.

Having been around the Bible my entire life, I knew about these spiritual truths in theory, but it amazed me to discover how applicable they were to my life. How had I missed all of this? I had been raised in a Christian home, went to a Christian high school, attended a Christian college, and had relied on God's protection during my three deployments to Iraq and Afghanistan. I knew about God and Jesus, but somehow, I had missed their significance. I could only conclude that my distance from God wasn't from lack of Christian influence. Rather, it was my own resistance to heed God's call.

Because I had grown up around God all of my life, I had become *tame* to His voice. Scriptural principles had become all head knowledge, and not heart knowledge. How many years had I wasted by not turning to God? It dawned on me that the more I had immersed myself in sin, the less I cared about the things of God. I had plenty of biblical knowledge, but very little belief. *Knowledge* can make a person sound intelligent, religious even, but belief will change one's life.

I was determined to rediscover the things of God. As I read more and more, I began to feel a deep sense of peace and calm coming over my soul. I began to breathe a little easier and even ventured to hope for the future. I felt as if I was drawing physical strength from the pages of my Bible, like I was shoring myself up for future days and battles ahead.

After reading Paul's letters for nearly an hour, I turned to the beginning of the New Testament, to the Gospel of Matthew. When I starting reading the passage with the Sermon on the Mount, I came across Jesus' words and what I now consider to be my life verse. Jesus said, *"Come to me, all you who are weary and burdened, and I will give you rest. Take my yoke upon you and learn from me, for I am gentle and humble in heart, and you will find rest for your souls"* (Matthew 11:28-29).

Once again, I became emotional and began to tear up. I could never have said it as well and complete as Jesus did. Those two verses summed up everything that I had been looking for. *Rest.* I had been running and searching for something greater for my entire life and I was exhausted. I needed true rest. I needed God's rest.

As the night came to an end, I thanked God for His mercy and grace. I felt humbled that He would give me another chance. But as wonderful as it felt to have new hope, I also had a feeling of unease. I knew that Friday afternoon would soon arrive to usher in the weekend and like so many times before, I wondered if I would succumb to the desire to drink.

Over the next two days I prayed for strength. I read the Bible. I listened to sermons. I tried to build up my courage. I tried positive self-talk. I did anything I could think of to fortify myself in preparation for the coming battle. Friday morning dawned bright and clear. All that morning I prayed for strength because I knew that in a few hours, the real battle would begin. Left to my own power, I knew that I would fail and I would be drinking again. I would have to rely on God to fight the battle for me.

As I left the office for the weekend, I prayed that God would grant me the strength and courage to drive past the liquor store on my way off base. I kept praying as I drove and as I passed the store, my hands shook and I felt the pull to go in, but I kept on driving. I left the base and drove onto the highway, thanking God for helping me bypass the liquor store. I arrived home and immediately went to my Bible to find Scripture verses to help me get through the afternoon and the evening.

I began to read from the book of Romans. I knew that Romans had good, practical advice and explained the sinful condition of man, so I thought it would be a good place to study. As I read Romans chapter 7, I zeroed in on the following passage:

> *"I do not really understand myself, for I want to do what is right, but I do not do it. Instead, I do what I hate. But if I know that what I am doing is wrong, this shows that I agree that the law is good. So I am not the one doing wrong, it is sin living in me that does it. And I know that nothing good lives in me, that is, in my sinful nature. I want to do what is right but I cannot. I want to do what is good, but I do not. I do not want to do what is wrong, but I do it anyway. But if I do what I do not want to do, I am not really doing wrong; it is sin living in me that does it. I have discovered this principle of life—that when I want to do what is right, I inevitably do what is wrong. I love God's law with all my heart. But there is another power within me that is at war with my mind. This power makes me a slave to the sin that is still within me. Oh what a miserable person I am! Who will free me from this life that is dominated by sin and death? Thank God! The answer is in Jesus Christ our Lord.*

> — ROMANS 7:15-25 NKJV

I had never heard it spelled out as clearly as that. The passage seemed to be talking about me exactly! I had loved and also hated alcohol for so long. I knew my self-destructive drinking habits were wrong, but I was powerless to stop them. I wanted to do what is right, but I could not seem to throw off my sinful tendencies. No matter how many times I tried to give it up, I never seemed to be able to do it. Did the passage mean that all my previous strategies were human efforts and doomed to fail? I think so.

I realized anew that the answer to my quandary was to rely on the power of Jesus Christ to come into my life, change my desires, and help me become a new person. At first, I struggled with the idea that Jesus Christ was the answer. After all, what does that really mean? How does belief in Christ translate into deliverance from temptation and tangible help in the moment? In time I would come to understand that Jesus Christ would give me the spiritual, physical, and emotional stamina to withstand my drinking desires and to eventually gain mastery over them. Just like the marathon runner who trains mile after mile in order to build his physical endurance, developing my relationship with Jesus Christ day after day would give me the spiritual endurance to beat my nemesis, and to choose the Lord over alcohol.

All that afternoon I continued to read the Bible. I took a break around 5 p.m. and went to the gym. I decided to pull up my pastor's sermons on podcast and listen during my workout. As it turned out, I ended up listening to a sermon where my pastor suggested writing down Scripture verses on 3x5 index cards. My pastor said he used the method himself to memorize verses from the Bible. He would write the verse itself on the front and the reference to the verse on the back. I thought that was a great idea and decided to write down verses to help me resist alcohol. Then when temptation came looking for me, I could pull the note cards out and have the power of the Scriptures at my fingertips.

Back at home, I went to my desk and pulled out a stack of 3x5 index cards. I decided to use the concordance in the back of my Bible to locate applicable verses. I was surprised at how many verses in the New Testament talked about resisting temptation and being filled with the Holy Spirit. I noted that the book of Galatians had quite a few good verses in it, so I started there.

My study Bible noted that one of the major themes in the book of Galatians is *freedom in Christ*. Right away I saw the significance of that. I had not felt free for many years. Freedom from alcohol was what I craved desperately. I finished reading the summary of Galatians and began to read the actual text. When I got to chapter 5, I began to write verses down on the cards.

The very first verse in Galatians 5 jumped off the page at me. *"It is for freedom that Christ has set us free. Stand firm, then, and do not let yourselves be burdened again by a yoke of slavery" (Galatians 5:1).* The verse rang loud and true. I had been in bondage for years, and I certainly didn't want to be enslaved again by alcohol. I wrote the verse on the front of the card and the reference on the back. Then I kept reading in Galatians and began to see the makings of a logical argument. The author of Galatians, Paul, wrote, *"You, my brothers and sisters, were called to be free. But do not use your freedom to indulge the flesh; rather, serve one another humbly in love"* (Galatians 5:13). I realized that God allows us freedom to pursue our own desires or to pursue Himself. Well, I had certainly decided to indulge myself rather than pursue Christ, serve others, or act in love toward the people around me. Paul finished the argument with verses 16-17, *"So I say, walk by the Spirit, and you will not gratify the desires of the flesh. For the flesh desires what is contrary to the Spirit, and the Spirit what is contrary to the flesh. They are in conflict with each other, so that you are not to do whatever you want" (Galatians 5:16-17).*

I wrote each of the verses down on my note cards and pondered as I wrote. The author of Galatians made the case that once we accept Christ into our lives and receive the Holy Spirit, our sinful nature does not vanish. It contends against the Holy Spirit. In the book of Galatians, Paul encourages us as believers to walk in the power of the Spirit in order to subdue our sinful nature and not give in to our desires. Any other defense against temptation is not reliable.

Once again, I was amazed at how little I knew the Scriptures. I knew all of the Bible stories told to children, like Noah's Ark, Daniel in the lion's den, and Jesus with his miracles and dying on the cross. But how little did I know about practical truths necessary to live the Christian life. Reading verses like these showed me that I had much to learn about Christian living.

As the evening progressed, the temptation to drink appeared out of nowhere; it came fast and furious and I started shaking all over. As I contended with the temptation, I continued to pray for strength, read my Bible, and quote the Scripture verses that I had written down on the note cards. In my search for applicable verses, I came across James 4:7, *"Therefore submit to God. Resist the devil and he will flee from you"* (NKJV). What a great verse. I wrote the verse on a new note card and put it on top of my stack. For the next 30 minutes I must have spoken that verse aloud no less than 20 times. And you know what? The desire for a drink never got past the strength of the Word of God that I was claiming for myself. I cooked dinner and watched a little TV and then continued to pray and read.

Around 11 p.m., I got into bed and read for a little while longer. I thanked God for His grace and helping me withstand the temptation, and then I fell into a deep and restful sleep. It was the first peaceful sleep that I had enjoyed in months.

As the days passed, I continued to read God's Word on a daily basis and I continued to not drink. As I kept placing my focus on my spiritual walk, I felt a power beyond myself giving me strength. The more I read the Bible and the closer I drew to the Lord, the more I felt Him drawing closer to me. Imagine it… the supreme creator of the universe would actually care about a mere, sinful human being such as me, after all the messed up things I had done. There is no logic in the concept. But it is so, and at long last I felt loved and forgiven and free. Finally, I felt rest.

17

I was enjoying my new period of sobriety and spiritual fervor, so I decided to use that momentum to make some other changes in my life. I had been through a string of relationships over the past few years that led nowhere, usually by my own undoing, and I was ready to find something real and meaningful. I felt such regret for how I had acted with some of the women. Now that I was sober, I wanted to approach things differently and live out my faith in terms of dating also. I was hopeful that my time had finally come. As if God was answering my prayers, I thought love arrived in February in a girl named Jolene.

We met online through one of the more popular dating sites. I made sure that my profile highlighted my Christian faith. I wanted to make a clean break from my old lifestyle and the kinds of women that I used to know. I definitely didn't want to be matched with a drinker or partier, or someone whose values didn't match my own. I wanted someone who would help strengthen my new-found commitment to faith, not someone who would tear it down piece by piece.

Jolene and I talked online for a couple weeks before deciding to meet. She was a Christian and conversation between us was easy. Right away we found many interests in common. Our spiritual and political views were closely aligned and we wanted the same things out of life. From what I could tell early on, we seemed to be a great match. The true test would be to meet her in person and see how we got along, but I felt pretty confident.

We met for the first time in late February at a local Starbucks in Falls Church, Virginia. I arrived first and took a seat towards the front on the left side and out of the direct view of the door. I wanted to make sure I saw her before she saw me. Call it insecurity, but without alcohol to make me bold, I felt vulnerable just sitting there in plain view. What if she was observing me from outside on the sidewalk and didn't like what she saw? What if I looked up from my phone and saw her looking at me with a deflated expression on her face? I didn't want that.

Ten minutes later, she walked through the door and I instantly liked what I saw. She had shoulder-length blonde hair, blue eyes, and was wearing a grey and red sweater dress with stockings, and she was pretty. She came over, greeted me warmly, and we got coffee together. I was nervous and shy and rambled on for a couple of minutes before I got my head out of the clouds, but our conversation went well. We sat and talked for thirty minutes or so over our coffees, then we left to go on our first date.

We had emailed back and forth about her love for cooking, so I took her to a nearby boutique spice store. I thought that was pretty creative. We browsed the aisles for a while and even bought a couple of spices. As we approached the checkout line, I asked if she would like to grab Italian for a late afternoon dinner. She said she'd love to, so we headed to one of my favorite Italian places in nearby Old Town, Alexandria.

Being in Old Town brought back memories from my time at The Basic School seven years earlier. Naturally, we stayed out of the bars I used to frequent, but I couldn't help but shudder when we walked past one of the Irish pubs that I'd known so well; after all, seven years wasn't that long ago. We enjoyed a nice meal and then walked around the city blocks and talked for a couple of hours. We kept finding new streets to explore and new things to talk about. I didn't want the afternoon to end.

Eventually it began to get dark and the temperature was dropping, so I drove her back to her car. Before she got in her car, I gave her a hug and asked her if I could see her again. She said, "I sure hope so" and then winked at me. Then she hopped in her car and drove away. I got back in my car and drove back to my condo feeling elated that things had gone so well. And I didn't even need alcohol to have a good time! I thought I was truly on the mend.

Jolene and I began seeing each other several times a week. As it turned out, we had more in common than I thought. We both attended the same church, although our paths had not crossed previously because she was in a small group on Sundays and I was volunteering each weekend in one of the ministries during that time. We decided to make church a focal point of our relationship and truly dedicate what we had to God and ask for His blessing. We felt we had something special and wanted to nurture it.

As our relationship continued, I knew I had to find a way to tell her about my drinking. I was afraid to bring it up and scare her off, but I couldn't keep it hidden forever. Things like that have a way of coming out.

After several dates, I found my lead-in. Jolene liked to order wine with dinner. After a month of dating, we were having dinner at a local restaurant and she ordered wine with her meal. She noticed that I didn't order any alcohol and she seemed to find it odd. I told her that I didn't drink *anymore* and that I was fine with water. She asked me if I used to drink, and so I began to tell her my story, albeit a watered-down version.

Jolene nodded in all the right places and reached across

the table and held my hand when I got to some of the harder parts. I was touched and relieved at the same time. She didn't seem to be getting up to run out of the restaurant. She seemed to accept my past and still like me for who I was.

THREE MONTHS CAME AND WENT AND I NEVER TOOK A DRINK. I continued to study the Word of God and I continued to pray. Jolene continued to drink wine with meals and sometimes in the evenings, but I abstained. However, as time went by, and as I got more used to my newly sober lifestyle, I began to do the spiritual things less and less. It wasn't a conscious decision on my part. Instead, life just seemed to get in the way.

Jolene and I were full steam ahead. I had decided to transition off active duty in the Marine Corps and I was busy interviewing with companies and planning my future career. My plan was to continue in the Marine Corps but in a reserves capacity. As time went by and I didn't drink, I figured that I had enough momentum and that I didn't need to protect myself as fervently as before. Eventually, I stopped keeping up with the spiritual basics that had finally brought me the freedom that I now enjoyed. I was surviving on willpower with a medium dose of God as backup.

I was foolish to think that I could let my guard down and the desire to drink would not come back. Just like when I was baptized in Afghanistan, I thought that since God had so graciously forgiven and restored me, that I was home free. As it turned out, God continued to be faithful, but I didn't.

By now it was the middle of April and Jolene happened to be out of town. I went about my weekend just like I usually did; nothing special. On Saturday afternoon, I left the gym and decided to run some errands. For some reason, around the middle of the afternoon, I began to reminisce about my drinking days. I'll never forget it.

I was walking along in a department store and I looked towards the front of the store and saw the sun shining in through the tinted glass. The window tint turned the sun a golden amber color and I immediately thought of the color of one my favorite beers. My body shivered and my heart began to race. Instead of recognizing the attack for what it was, I continued to recall the "good times" that alcohol had given me. I thought more and more about my drinking days and remembered how much I loved the taste of alcohol and how I missed the feeling of being drunk.

Rather than praying for strength and courage, I began to think about what it would be like to drink again. Would it really be so terrible? I had been sober for three months. What was one night? Surely, I could drink this one time and get back on track the following Monday.

Wait, what was I thinking!? Was I really going to drink again!? I shook my head to clear the thoughts and felt shame that the thoughts had even crossed my mind. God had been so gracious to me. How could I go back?

I left that particular store and went on to the next one, but the desire and impulse to drink hit me again even stronger and would not let up. I kept fighting the thoughts, but my attempts turned into half-hearted dodges. Finally, at the end of my errands, I found myself in a liquor store buying a bottle of scotch and a six-pack of beer. In some ways, it seemed surreal to me. Like I was in a vision or parallel universe and it wasn't really me doing it all.

I fought the traffic to get home and cracked the first beer as soon as I walked in the door. Just like before, I began to put the groceries away and unwind from the day with a bottle in my hand. The beer tasted magical. I felt like a parched traveler tasting that first drink of cold, refreshing water.

I continued to do chores around my house and drink my

way through the six-pack. After two hours or so, the beer was gone and I opened the bottle of scotch. I put some ice cubes in a rocks glass and poured myself a few fingers. I still knew what I was doing was wrong, to let myself go down this road after all I'd been through, but the beer helped to deaden my guilt. I thought, *what gives, I've been liberated from alcohol and I can have a few drinks.* The scotch went down my throat and exploded like fire in my stomach. It tasted amazing.

I awoke sometime in the wee hours of the morning, totally disoriented and inebriated. Somehow, I'd ended up in the bathtub with a spilled drink all over myself. My head throbbed from where I must have hit the hard tiles on my way down. Shards of glass speckled the tub and tile floor from the broken rocks glass. It took me several minutes to muster the coordination to get up out of the tub and pull myself together. I turned on the shower, cleaned myself up, and crawled into bed. I was still too drunk to think or do anything beyond that.

The following morning, I felt ashamed of myself and angry. The amount of guilt I felt was overwhelming. I had been professing to anyone who asked that I had supposedly turned over a new chapter in my life and here I was, right back to my old ways. Three months of sobriety and I had thrown it away for what? An evening of scotch and beer and a day-long hangover? I even began to wonder if any of my spiritual experience had been real or not. Had God really helped me or was I just riding a wave of temporary motivation, one that was now crashing, dejected, along the beach?

No, I determined that it was real. I had been sober for three months. That was real. I knew that God had forgiven me because I could *feel* it. That was real. I reasoned that I had just become careless. The enemy had been waiting for his chance and I had given it to him. Just when I wasn't looking for him, he punched me right between the eyes and knocked me down. I resolved right then and there that it would not happen again. I got back into the Bible, praying throughout my day, and quoting my Scripture verses when tempting thoughts crossed my mind. In doing so, I realized how much I had missed the fellowship with God that I had enjoyed earlier in the year. I continued to keep up the spiritual disciplines and logged another month of clean time.

But then, life got in the way once again. Things with Jolene were going well, and we were constantly out and about to dinner, to wineries, to parties. I continued to be distracted by her and with building a new career. As spring turned into summer, I began to take a drink here or two drinks there, sometimes with Jolene, sometimes without. My mind lied to me with the notion that it was controlled, social drinking now, not the unbridled type of drinking that I did before. Jolene also maintained her steady state of social drinking. In fact, it seemed that alcohol was always around.

Looking back, that should have been a red flag for me. Back when I was building my online dating profile, I remember hoping to meet a Christian girl who would encourage me and support me in my efforts *not* to drink. Instead, times with Jolene started to center more and more on activities where alcohol would be present. My intense binges didn't return, but the drinks became more frequent. I tried to juggle my spiritual commitments, my relationship with Jolene, and the ever-building pull back into my old way of life. Alcohol was everywhere, and the more I tried to stick to my resolve, the more I continued to backslide.

Over the next six months, I went back and forth. One drink became three. Three drinks turned into a bottle. A bottle turned into drunk. I would drink Friday nights and then stay sober for the rest of the weekend. I would be drunk for a weekend and then be sober for a month. There wasn't any logic or pattern to it.

The entire time, I wrestled with guilt. I reflected back on that pivotal point in my life the year before, and *I knew* the spiritual basics and how to break free from alcohol's hold on my life. So why was I not doing the basics? Why did I keep putting God off for yet another day? He had forgiven me and shown me how to get right and *stay right* with Him. I had given Him complete control of my life for a little while, but apparently I reserved the right to take it back when it suited me. I followed God when it worked and drank when temptations came along.

AMIDST THIS BACKDROP, THE MONTH OF JUNE ARRIVED AND things with Jolene had deepened to the point that I was planning to ask her to marry me. We were only four months into our relationship, but it felt like we'd known each other forever. I was confident that our relationship was ordained by God. I talked with her father and mother and they gave me their blessing to ask for her hand in marriage. I purchased a beautiful ring and started planning out my proposal.

Jolene loved butterflies and flowers, so I decided to propose to her at the botanical gardens in Washington D.C. On a warm day in June, we walked the garden and I scouted out a very quiet corner of the garden where we could sit down, and after some conversation, I got down on one knee and proposed. And she said yes! We were so happy together and we began to share hopes and dreams and romanticize about what our married life would be like.

That summer we planned our wedding and I continued to interview for jobs for when I would leave active duty. Neither activity left much time for drinking, so I was able to stay sober most of the time, minus the occasional bender. Although I had revealed my past struggles with alcohol to Jolene, in the few months that we had been dating there had only been a few serious drinking episodes. Since she also enjoyed drinking quite often, my new fiancée's level of concern wasn't too high.

By that June I had secured a job, and I began to breathe a little easier in that regard. I was on Marine Corps terminal leave and wasn't due to start my new job until September. That left a lot of free time, and I ended up using some of that time for drinking. In fact, I totally dropped my guard. I wasn't reading the Bible daily, I wasn't praying, and I wasn't thinking about being a spiritual leader to my fiancée. Rather than getting back to God, I filled up the empty hours by working out at the gym, playing golf, spending time with Jolene, and yes, drinking.

I ended up getting drunk one night around the second week of July. I had woken up that morning feeling well and refreshed. I began my day without even thinking about alcohol. I had some errands to run that morning, several calls to make, and then I wanted to work out at the gym. My day went along just fine and by the time the afternoon rolled around, I had worked out and was browsing the grocery aisles, picking up items to make dinner that night. In fact, I even called my fiancée at her office, just to hear her voice.

As I walked the aisles, I ended up near the meat counter; the wine aisle was one row over. I thought to myself, *why not?* I can get a bottle or two and put it in a kitchen cabinet for later on, like when I host a dinner party or something like that. So I picked out my two favorite bottles of wine and continued on. Somehow, several specialty beers also found their way into my cart.

I drove home and put my groceries away and began to do some chores. Later in the evening, I decided to pour myself a glass of wine. One glass became two, and two glasses became a bottle. One bottle turned into two, and then I opened some of the beer that I bought. I only had a few specialty beers in the house and I knew that I would end up staggering down to the corner store for more. As I thought about getting more alcohol, the old familiar urge and tension began to come back into my head. I could literally feel it spreading through my brain, commanding me to go get more alcohol. Just like old times, I was powerless against it, and soon, I found myself walking down to the store.

As I walked, I could almost hear the enemy sweet-talking me by saying *"Jordan, you are only going to get a six-pack. Nothing more. Don't worry about this."* That thought provided a little relief, but when I finally got to the store, another thought flickered through my head. *"Well, Jordan, since you are already here, why not make it a twelve-pack? At least it will save you a trip in coming back down here for more."* What a great idea. It made perfect sense to me. So, I grabbed a twelve-pack and a couple of snacks and started back towards my condo.

I got back to the house and within two hours, the twelve-pack was gone and another thought went through my head. *"Jordan, it is only 10 p.m. and you are already drunk, but there is too much night left and you are out of alcohol. Go down and get more and this time make it a twenty-four pack."* I made the trip to the store and back in about thirty minutes, put the beer in the fridge, and proceeded to get really drunk. I must have passed out on the couch sometime in the night because when I woke up, it was 3 a.m. Now that I was wide awake, I decided to keep on drinking. I mean, why not? I had already blown it. I was still drunk from the night before. I might as well continue.

As daylight began to creep through the windows, somehow, I had the presence of mind that I needed to quit and get some rest. But, before I got into bed, Jolene called while on her way to work to say good morning. Foolishly, I picked up the phone. The words, "Hey babe" came out of my mouth so slurred and sluggish that there was absolutely no way I could hide it. She instantly exploded on me. To this day, I cannot remember much of what she said, but I was positive that I had upset her deeply. My drinking had caused her minor hurt and irritation before, but this was different. She was really upset and hurt, maybe for the final time. The last words she spoke to me before she hung up were, "Get some sleep, we will talk about this when you are sober." With that, I got up off the couch and staggered into my bedroom, flopped on the bed, and was asleep within minutes.

When I woke up that afternoon, I was groggy and fuzzy, but far from being drunk. I was so ashamed of myself that I couldn't even look at myself in the mirror. I couldn't believe that I was back in the same exact place as other relationships, yet again, wondering what excuse to make and questioning whether the relationship could be saved. I kept thinking over and over again that I had finally gone and crossed a line and that my fiancée was going to call off the wedding. I thought that I had lost her forever. I had no idea what I would say to her. What could I say? "I'm sorry"? That wouldn't cut it. Fast talking and empty promises weren't going to be good enough either. I was too embarrassed to call her, so I texted her instead to break the ice. She said she wasn't interested in seeing me that evening, but maybe the following day.

The next day, she called and said she wanted to see me that night to talk about our future. I figured she was going to call off the wedding. I remember driving up I-95 towards her house with knots in my stomach. I got to her house and we sat outside on her back porch. We hardly even spoke. She just looked at me with this sad expression on her face. I could tell she was struggling with her emotions. My own feelings were swirling just below the surface.

I didn't know what to say or how to express what I felt. I just knew that I was disgusted with myself. I didn't try to argue with anything she said and I didn't try to fill up the silence with a bunch of empty promises. Instead I just stared at the deck table and responded to her when it seemed appropriate; a "hmm" here, an affirmative nod there. Her words revealed that she still loved me. While she couldn't just turn that off at will, she was far from happy with me. Her biggest fear was that we'd get married and my drinking would continue. She wasn't thrilled about being married to a drunk, but she also didn't say anything about calling off the wedding. We parted ways that night having made a little progress, but things between us were far from ok.

We were both invested enough to work through the issue, but it took several weeks for the ice to thaw. The busyness of our lives helped. There was still so much to do. I needed to start my new job and we had a wedding to finish planning. So, we settled into a truce of sorts and finished out the summer.

Things were finally back on an upswing when September rolled around. By now, most of the wedding details were set. They had to be because Jolene was going to England on a business trip with her company for three months, right before our wedding date in December. She wouldn't come back until a few days before our wedding day, so all the major pieces had to be decided ahead of time and then it would be up to me to see to the final details.

Jolene left for England on a Friday afternoon in early September. I had started my new job a few weeks before, so I wasn't able to see her off at the airport. She called me that afternoon as I was driving home from the office. We made small talk for a while and I could tell she was excited about traveling overseas for such a long time. I put up a brave front, but the truth was that I was going to miss her, and I was more than a little scared about the temptations of drinking without her there to keep me in check.

Jolene settled into her temporary duties in England and I went to work each day and continued to finalize details for our December wedding. I quickly discovered that without her presence, it was harder and harder to say no to drinking. So hard in fact that I lost the fight each weekend.

I wrestled with many things that fall. I was struggling to find a new identity that wasn't tied to active duty in the Marine Corps. Dissatisfaction with what I was doing made me less motivated to excel at my job. Underperforming caused me to feel guilty which in turn made me want to turn to my constant friend, alcohol. I ended up drinking to excess each weekend and sometimes during the week as well. I found myself using alcohol to cope all over again.

Jolene and I traded emails back and forth every day. We also talked on the phone once or twice each week, usually on a weeknight. That made it easier to hide what I was doing on the weekends. I put on a good show, but I think she could sense that I was getting into drinking more than she would have liked. For some reason, she never asked me about drinking, so at least I didn't have to lie.

18

The end of my drinking finally came when my marriage fell apart.

Jolene and I were married in December of that year. We chose to have the wedding ceremony and reception in a historic inn located to the west of Washington D.C., in the beautiful horse and wine countryside of Middleburg, Virginia. The inn was built in 1726 and the structure still boasted all of the original hardwood floors, windows, and fixtures. The walls were paneled in dark mahogany, fireplaces crackled in all the rooms, and romantic candlelight illuminated the inn. The entire town of Middleburg was decorated in the Christmas spirit. Wreaths hung on every door and greenery draped nearly every business. Lights twinkled in the trees that lined the quaint main street and all the shop windows were bedecked in Christmas trimmings. The wedding was intimate, with just our families and closest friends in attendance, but it was a beautiful wedding and everyone enjoyed themselves immensely.

The next few weeks after the wedding were busy ones for my new wife and me. We decided to wait on a honeymoon since we had rented a new townhouse earlier in the month and we had a move-in date scheduled for the first of the New Year. For the next two weeks after the wedding, we scrambled to secure moving trucks and pack up the belongings from our respective homes. Then moving day arrived and we loaded up the moving truck with her belongings and then my own, and drove over to our new townhouse. There was so much to unload. Freezing rain was coming down hard that night and it took us nearly 12 hours to unload everything and finally return the moving truck. We came back to the house, freezing and exhausted, and collapsed into bed.

We enjoyed our first few months of married life. Both of us stayed busy with our respective jobs and we attended church on the weekends. Slowly but surely, we unpacked and arranged our townhouse while we also adjusted to living life together. Even though we had spent quite a bit of time together during our brief dating relationship, nothing is quite the same as truly living with someone, especially when it comes to the everyday, practical side of life. We learned a lot about each other and compromised where it seemed appropriate.

Early on in our marriage, I really tried to control the presence of alcohol in my daily life. Sometimes we had wine with meals or beers with friends, but for the most part, I was able to use willpower to stay sober. In fact, during those first few months I think I was drunk just a handful of times. My drinking represented a minor source of irritation for my wife, but for the most part, I was able to keep my problem under control.

As winter turned into spring, however, my drinking became worse. I worked long hours during the week trying to build my new career outside of the Marine Corps, and when Friday night came around, the only thing I wanted to do was relax at home, cook dinner, spend time with my wife, and have a couple of drinks. Or many drinks. At first, my wife and I drank together and it was enjoyable to relax in that manner.

But within a month or two, my drinking pace outmatched hers. While she could stop at two or three drinks, I found that I needed at least six or seven drinks. When that wasn't enough, I steadily added more and more drinks to the mix. What started out innocently enough in terms of relaxing together and ushering in the weekend soon developed into a major problem between us.

My drinking took a further turn for the worse about five months into our marriage, during Memorial Day weekend. Jolene and I had the opportunity to go down to the Outer Banks of North Carolina to celebrate the holiday. We ended up joining my brother, his wife, and another couple at a beach house for four days of rest and relaxation. The purpose of the vacation was to relax and spend time with each other and our spouses, but what we ended up doing was partying like when we were younger.

The refrigerator was stocked with so much beer and wine that the door could hardly close. From the moment that we walked into the beach house to the moment we all left, we were drinking. If we went down to the beach during the day, we were drinking. If we were grilling food for dinner, we were drinking. If we were playing card games together in the evening, we were drinking. And I drank more than anyone. I didn't even go to bed some nights, but instead stayed up after everyone else fell asleep and drank more beer. I would end up being awake all night, reading to myself with alcohol in hand, and then would cook breakfast for everyone the morning after. Then in the evenings, I would grill steaks and hot dogs for everyone in the evenings while all the while pounding more drinks.

One evening I was so drunk that I accidentally sliced one of my fingers to the bone while I was putting hot dogs on the grill. Jolene had to drive me 40 minutes up the coast to get stitches in order to stop the bleeding. She ripped my head off the whole way to the hospital about my drinking and barely spoke to me on the way back to the beach house. After four days, it was time to call a halt to the party and head back to Virginia.

Jolene never came right out and said it, but I sensed that she began to look at me differently after we returned home. Before the vacation, I was her husband who occasionally drank too much. She could shrug it off, make up excuses for my behavior to her friends, and not worry too much about it. But after Memorial Day, I think she began to look at me as her husband the alcoholic, and I think she seriously began to wonder what her life would be like years into the future if things kept going as they seemed to be.

To make matters worse, I was realizing that Jolene also had some behaviors that bothered me. One of them was the friends that she kept who were anything but positive influences in her life. Her girlfriends were like sisters to her and encouraged her to not put up with my drinking, while at the same time suggesting outlets for her frustrations in the form of partying and drinking of her own. Another of those outlets were other men in her life. When my drinking began to worsen, Jolene chose to spend more and more time with her guy friends and male co-workers. Often, she would return to our house very late in the evening. I'd ask her where she'd been and she would tell me that she and her guy friends had been out at happy hours, visiting local wineries, or getting a late-night dinner together. Of course, this bothered me, but because of my drinking, she acted like I had no grounds to lodge any complaints. My drinking absolved her of any bad moral behavior of her own.

More and more, I felt like I was at the bottom of her priority list. Her friends always came first. With all of the late nights she spent with them, I began to think that their relationship had crossed the line. Even though I never formally accused her of having an affair, I very much suspected that it was occurring. It was a hard thing for me to wrap my head around, especially because I partially blamed myself.

The wedge between us drew us further and further apart. Jolene increasingly didn't have time for church activities, and both of us put God on the back burner. She threw herself into her work and turned to her friends for comfort, while I increasingly hung out with MY old friend, alcohol.

To make matters worse, Jolene took several trips that summer to visit friends and family in her hometown, plus a couple of trips overseas for her job. Her multiple day absences gave me a prime opportunity to drink. Each time she left town, I went back to my old routine of stocking up on booze and getting drunk. I pounded alcohol all weekend and sobered up in time to pick her up from the airport. Before leaving for the airport, I was always careful to get rid of the evidence. I cleaned up the house and took all of the beer cans to the trash. I even paid for most of the alcohol with cash so that she wouldn't see the transactions on our bank statements. But even though I was careful to hide my behavior, she was no fool. She knew what I had been doing while she was gone. But I wondered what she had been doing as well.

Summer turned into fall and fall turned into winter, and the rift between us got wider. My drinking angered her and I was frustrated with her about many of the poor lifestyle choices she was making. I had a running debate with myself, asking whether or not I had made a huge mistake in marrying her in the first place. At the same time, I couldn't fault her completely; after all, I was drinking and I was hurting her. She did have good reason to draw away from me. Unfortunately, we didn't humble ourselves before God and draw strength from Him to rebuild our fledgling marriage. Instead, we turned to our vices and continued to drift further apart.

By the time our one-year anniversary came around, we were living in a new house. It was a very large home and much of our spare time was spent painting, organizing our belongings, and making the place our own. The home renovations gave me enough distraction to stay sober for weeks at a time. By then, my wife and I had settled into an unspoken uncertainty about our future.

Subconsciously, we both knew that we couldn't continue along the present course, but neither of us really knew what to do about it. Thoughts of divorce were in the back of our minds, even though we never spoke about it openly. I know she didn't think I'd ever stop drinking and I was pretty sure she was having affairs behind my back. She could hardly speak to me without scorn or ridicule. I felt like I deserved everything she dished my way. I didn't know how to communicate with her. We were so close when we started and I remembered how excited we were to be planning our future together. How had we come to this?

It wasn't until late January that the distance and frustration in my heart began to dissipate and I began to warm back up to the things of God and my wife. I'm not entirely sure what brought on the change. Perhaps it was foreseeing the demise of my marriage in the not-too-distant future unless I could turn things around. Maybe it was my mind fast-forwarding to a lifetime of loneliness and regret if I squandered yet another wake-up call and lost yet another relationship. This time, it would be my wife.

I had sought out the help of a Christian counselor for my drinking a month or two before and his guidance and support had slowly been taking hold, so perhaps it was the Holy Spirit having an opening in my life again. The important thing is that my heart began to change. I began to have real regret for my drinking and my failure to be a godly husband. I began to read the Bible again and also pray consistently, the same spiritual basics that always brought me back into my walk with the Lord. Little by little, my drinking became less and less and I became intentional in looking for ways to rebuild my marriage.

The godly wisdom and spiritual prodding of my counselor was critical in my fight to get sober and try to save my marriage. I offered to bring Jolene with me to my counseling sessions, sort of a hybrid drinking and marriage rebuilding session. She attended two or three sessions with me, but quickly tired of hearing the counselor mentor us from a biblical perspective. She soon stopped going all together. Her heart had grown cold and callous to the things of God. For weeks, I kept trying to do what I could to save our marriage, but unfortunately, it was too little too late.

I arrived home from work one evening in February to find Jolene sobbing on the living room couch. I asked her what was wrong, but all she could do was look at me with a sad expression on her face. She asked if we could "talk." I knew enough about "talking" to expect the worst, but I couldn't refuse her. Perhaps to gear up for the conversation ahead, I suggested that we go out to dinner and find a quiet booth. I think she preferred to stay at home that night, but she agreed. We changed clothes and headed to a nearby steakhouse for dinner. The host seated us at a booth near the kitchen, in the same booth where we'd had one of our early dates. I couldn't help but notice the irony.

We both took our time looking over the menu. I welcomed any distraction that might delay the inevitable. After several uncomfortable minutes, we placed our orders and then Jolene started off by saying, "So...." and continued that she'd been thinking about our marriage and how unfulfilled she was. She wasn't happy about the distance between us. She wasn't happy about how much I drank. She wasn't satisfied with our level of interaction or closeness. She was upset that I wasn't clicking with her girl and guy friends. In short, she just wasn't happy with me as a husband. She expected that our marriage would be this wonderful, continually-happy experience. The longer she stayed with me, the more she realized that she was miserable and she wanted out.

Her words cut, even though they didn't truly come as a shock. She said that she wasn't in love with me as a marriage partner and that she didn't even love me as a person. Marrying me had been a huge mistake. After less than a year and a half of marriage, she wanted a divorce. In fact, she wanted to make a complete break with her entire way of life, Christianity included. No amount of counseling or promises of sobriety were going to change her mind. She wanted to be free and to do things her way.

Jolene seemed to be full of plans already. She told me she'd grown restless and complacent with her career. She wanted to reinvent herself and not waste one more minute of her life sitting behind a desk. She wanted to travel and experience things. She also said she was through with Christianity. Even though her parents were devout Christians and had raised her to be the same, she said she had always felt she was living their faith, not her own. And based on recent events, she was pretty sure that there was no one listening on the other end of her prayers. So she was done with that way of life. She thought God was a myth.

I remember not knowing what to say in response. I wasn't surprised to hear her ask for a divorce, even if I was taken aback by all she said about our marriage and about God. We had been struggling for the last several months, and yet it didn't make her words hurt any less. We muddled through dinner with stilted conversation. Any overtures to work on our marriage or inspire hope for our future were refuted. The most troubling aspect was her desire to walk away from her faith. I didn't know if it was possible to rekindle her love for me or for God.

≈

THE MORNING AFTER MY WIFE ASKED FOR A DIVORCE WAS A strange one for me. I didn't feel all that different somehow, and yet I knew we were facing a huge crossroads in our marriage and in our lives. Maybe I was in a state of shock and reality hadn't set in yet. I do remember having the notion that perhaps our marriage wasn't completely over; perhaps she was lashing out and wasn't really serious about leaving. Maybe it wasn't too late to fix our marriage and I could win her back.

Since the state of Virginia requires married couples with no children to go through a six-month period of separation before a final divorce is granted, I figured I had six months to save our marriage. Until then, we agreed to live in different parts of our large house, but I still hoped that we could work through our problems and save our relationship.

During our separation, I continued meeting with my Christian counselor. Now faced with my marriage failing, I was fervent in my efforts to face my issues head-on. Those weekly counseling sessions kept me sane. I brought up my marriage troubles during the sessions, along with my alcohol problem. Rather than just treating the symptoms, at last I was beginning to deal with the underlying root cause of my drinking. All along, I'd been attempting to control my drinking through my own willpower, but that could only last so long. Now, I was seeing my drinking as a manifestation of a spiritual problem.

The recurring theme in my life until this point was not giving God full lordship over my life and taking my relationship with God for granted. When things got unbearable, I would pray and do "Christian things" for a short while, but as soon as I got on my feet, I let those disciplines slide and my relationship with God went onto the back burner. I would start relying on myself more and more, and on God less and less, and pretty soon I was back to where I had started. A broken, drunken mess.

My counselor helped me dig into the "why," or in other

words, the motivations of my heart. He didn't dispense the practical, man-made steps to stop drinking; instead he prompted me to look at the person in the mirror and examine the core issues deep inside. The counseling sessions helped me realize that I was dealing with an identity problem. My entire identity was wrapped up in alcohol; it had become my crutch, my confidence, my *idol*. I considered myself a nobody without alcohol there to boost me up, yet I also felt like a failure and a drunk when I gave in to its influence. It hadn't seemed possible to forge an identity as anything else or to go through life alone without alcohol. Until now.

I'll never forget the day after my very last drink. It was the 19th of April, and there was nothing particularly special about the day itself, other than the sun was bright and the weather was warm. But *something* about the day seemed significant. I had been wasted over the weekend and by now it was such an old, overrated experience for me. I wanted to be done with the hassle and with the aftermath of drinking. I was so tired of the warring emotions inside. My thoughts flickered to the passage of Scripture that had been particularly meaningful to me during my last period of sobriety a couple years back, the words spoken by Jesus Himself: *"Come to me, all you who are weary and burdened, and I will give you rest. Take my yoke upon you and learn from me, for I am gentle and humble in heart, and you will find rest for your souls. For my yoke is easy and my burden is light"* (Matthew 11:28-30). I felt weary and burdened just like the verse described, and oh, how I yearned for rest for my soul!

Things had been slowly building to this point over the course of years. Being on the brink of losing my marriage was one more thing added to the heap. Through one heartbreak after another, God had seen fit to overturn my life. Now, he had finally convinced me that He was the means to rebuild it and that a new outcome was possible. Somehow, I knew that April 19 was *the* day, the true start of my sobriety.

When I told my counselor that I had claimed April 19 as

the first day of my sobriety, he was thrilled and encouraged me to build on the momentum. I took it day-by-day, week-by-week, staying connected to God and taking nothing for granted. I continued to see my counselor regularly and worked to deepen my relationship with God. I found that sobriety was the resulting outcome of putting God first in my life.

While I tried to rebuild my life, Jolene seemed intent on destroying hers. She partied hard and came home late many nights. She was still distant from me and from God. But, in June of that year, I thought we hit a breakthrough. She'd been showing signs of remorse for wanting to end our marriage. We even had several late-night conversations that led me to believe she was coming around to wanting to give our marriage a second chance. Perhaps she was seeing some of the changes in my life and that they were real. Maybe her parents were encouraging her to not give up on her marriage. Whatever the reason, I wanted to engage with her and try to find common ground to rebuild.

She had been seeing a private counselor on her own, someone she trusted to give her an unbiased opinion and guidance on what to do next. Upon her counselor's recommendation, Jolene invited me to attend a session with her, and I gladly went. The counselor talked to us for thirty minutes and then said, "Listen, I see people in my office all the time who are broken, with their marriages falling apart. You two can easily fix this. You just have to open your hearts and want it." I was ecstatic. Finally! A professional counselor that Jolene trusted was agreeing with me. But I could tell that Jolene was torn.

I think a part of her wanted to reconcile because she knew it was the right thing to do, but I think another part of her was skeptical of whether she even wanted that. I had been sober for a few weeks now, but she had no guarantee that it was going to last. She had decided to create her own pleasurable life through whatever means were available, since I had let her down. She would have preferred the therapist to validate her desire to leave her dirt bag husband behind and pursue her own life to the fullest.

After we left the therapist's office, we grabbed dinner at a local restaurant and talked about the counseling session. We discussed what life would be like if we were to reconcile. There were positives and negatives, but overall it was a hopeful conversation. For the first time in months, I felt like there was a real chance that we could get back together. I drove us back to the house feeling relieved.

The following month, Jolene had another business trip in England that was scheduled to last several weeks. I was apprehensive about her going because I was afraid we would lose any momentum that we had. If she went to England, she could party and link up with any number of guys and I would never know. But I decided that the only way to test her heart would be to observe how she acted when she returned. All I could control was *me* at this point. For the first time, I did not view her absence as an opportunity to get completely wasted. Instead, I poured into my relationship with God, kept up my sessions with my Christian counselor, maintained my sobriety, and each day felt a little stronger.

Jolene got through her trip and returned home the last week of July. When she got back, my worst fears were realized. She was aloof and callous and wanted very little do with me. Any progress that we had made previously was gone. Whatever had happened during her trip did not bring us closer together. My deflation was further reinforced when she approached me that August and said that she was going to find a place of her own with a girlfriend of hers. Her meaning was loud and clear. She didn't feel comfortable pursuing her pleasures with me under the same roof. My presence was a continual thorn in her side and she wanted to be free to see whoever she wanted and do whatever she wanted. Once she left the house, I knew all hope of reconciliation was lost.

We had very little contact that fall. The only time we spoke was when a decision needed to be made about the house or other joint assets. Our conversations were short and terse; all business, no warmth. The holidays that year were quite dismal for me. I was still processing my emotions and having to accept the sad truth that my wife wanted nothing more to do with me and had completely moved on. In January, she called to tell me that the divorce would be final the following week. She also told me she was resigning her job that next summer and leaving the country to live abroad. She wasn't coming back. The last time I saw her was when she came to drop off a car that we owned together. I never saw her again.

WHEN I TRULY REALIZED THAT MY MARRIAGE WAS OVER, MY entire world turned upside down. In the past, I would have drowned my sorrows in alcohol. In fact, the thought became very tempting. However, I knew that drinking would provide only a brief, temporary relief, and after sobering up, I would still have to face the fact that my marriage was over. Because of that, I knew that my sobriety had to prevail this time. No more games, no more dabbling, no more half measures. I had a choice to make. I could continue in my old ways and face total devastation, or I could finally get clean once and for all.

Of course, I knew how to do this. I had done it two years before, even though it had been short-lived. I knew that I had to keep on giving God total control, 100% of the time, and reorient my life and purpose to be living for Him. The theory was air-tight; it was the execution that gave me doubts. I knew I could do it for short periods of time, but could I live another fifty years without taking a drink, solely by relying on God's power and grace alone? The idea overwhelmed me, but I knew that it was my only way forward if I hoped to be free.

Those next several weeks were some of the hardest weeks of my life. Sure, I had been through grueling boot camp and officer's candidate school, and then gone to war several times, but this was different. Those were physical and mental difficulties that could be overcome through training and determination. My addiction to alcohol was a much deeper thing. Drinking had become an emotional, spiritual snare for me, and well, it was *my thing*. Alcohol was my go-to, my comfort, my safe place. It was where I found solace, albeit the wrong kind. I had turned to alcohol instead of God, instead of my wife, instead of role models, instead of other Christians, every time. The idea of not having alcohol in my life was hard to wrap my mind around. But I desperately wanted that new identity, the one not defined by my addiction or by my failures. I didn't want to BE a drunk any longer.

I resolved in my heart to turn my mind and attention to God every single day. I chose to spend time on things that put God first. I made it a point to read passages in my Bible regularly and soak in what Scripture had to say. I spent a lot of time in the books of Romans and Galatians because of their emphasis on using God's power to overcome temptations and sin in our lives. I dug into the archives of my pastor's sermons and listened to one sermon after the other. I kept myself reflecting on spiritual things intermittently throughout the day. I also prayed with more intention, calling on God casually and frequently as I went about my business.

These new priorities of mine didn't inspire a heart change overnight. I still had the desire to drink. I didn't *feel* close to God at first even though I was mentally choosing to draw close, and it's not as if I felt a sudden supernatural presence that defied the call of the bottle.

No, in many ways I felt very much the same as before. But I did these things in order to build spiritual discipline. I sincerely believe that the reason I relapsed on my sobriety two years previously was because I had become spiritually complacent. I figured that God had done His part and I had done my part and that I was "cured" and out of danger. But because we are born with sin natures, we will always be prone to sin. Sin is what comes naturally to us, and with a little neglect, we quickly find ourselves mired again in sinful behavior.

With my deepening focus on spiritual things, I knew I needed to surround myself with positive, godly influences. I renewed my commitment to attend church and began to look for opportunities to volunteer, especially on the weekends. One of the ways I had grown complacent previously was to have too much free time on my hands. When I had a weekend full of empty hours staring me in the face, my resolve tended to weaken and I'd end up filling the time with drinking.

So, I found a ministry at church that needed some of the skills I had learned in the Marines and I volunteered. Most of the other volunteers were younger to middle aged men. What's more, they were godly men. They proved it in the way they acted and spoke. I considered this to be a blessing because having godly men in my life wasn't something I was used to. I became very close with some of them and shared my story and the trials that I had experienced in recent years. Many of the men offered emotional support and strength in a rugged sort of way. I welcomed their encouragement and they kept me honest about my behavior and held me accountable when necessary.

During this time, I also continued to see my Christian counselor. We met no less than once every two weeks, usually more. It was not uncommon for me to be sitting on the couch in his office each Saturday afternoon at 5 pm. His wisdom and guidance helped me to strengthen my faith and my resolve to stay sober. I continued to stay on my guard towards alcohol and I fought every day for my sobriety. I stayed away from bars; I refused to go have beers with "the guys" or venture out to happy hours. If family members were having a drink, I stayed on the opposite side of the room. At the grocery store, I refused to walk down the beer and wine aisle. Even the smell of alcohol on someone's breath reminded me of where I came from and what I was striving to overcome.

I kept this all up day after day, week after week. As my spiritual discipline grew, I discovered that it was easier and easier to fight off the urge to drink. Just as you train your muscles to grow and become stronger, I was learning to train and build my spiritual muscles. The more I practiced reading the Bible, meditating on what I had read and praying throughout my day, the easier it became to be consistent doing those things. And the easier it became to resist drinking. My mindset shifted. My thoughts weren't preoccupied with alcohol and how long it had been since my last drink. No, my focus was shifting to God and thinking on the things and ways of God. *What would God have me do? Where does He want me to go from here? What does He still want to teach me?*

Praying consistently began to open me up to a whole new way of communicating with God. I had sat in church for most of my life and had heard the complete spectrum of prayers— long, laborious prayers that never seemed to end and prayers that were short and sweet. Some prayers seemed to be scripted and too perfect in their holiness, while other prayers truly flowed from the heart. My prayer life had never been strong, but now as my prayer life deepened, I found that the best kind of prayer that worked for me was rapid fire prayer. I would send up quick one to two-minute prayers about whatever I was encountering during the day. The prayer didn't even have to be about anything all that important, but I was learning the process of constant reliance on God for even the smallest things in life.

I prayed for parking spaces at the gym. I prayed about uncomfortable situations at work. I prayed for wisdom in making certain financial decisions. Later on, after my wife left, I prayed for the loneliness I was encountering in my newly single status. I prayed for continual strength and courage to not take that next drink. And God answered. He didn't answer in an audible or visual way; instead, He gave me enough courage, emotional endurance and grace to make it through that moment, that hour, and that day without taking a drink.

To combat the thoughts of alcohol, I was choosing to think on the Lord's things with my mind, and in doing so, my heart was also coming around. I was feeling and enjoying God's presence more and more. I was truly relying on His supernatural strength and believing in my heart that He was with me. Rather than just head knowledge and going through the motions of my faith, it was becoming heart knowledge. For the first time in a long while, I was truly communing with God. He was sharing my day. I was finally ready to be in the long-term relationship with my Savior that He had always intended. I was inviting Him to be present with me, and He met me where I was and showed me grace. Amazing grace! How sweet the sound!

Before I knew it, I had managed to string thirty days of sobriety together. I was ecstatic, although I tried not to be overly confident. I still remembered the past times of relapsing on my sobriety. However, I began to have real hope that I could truly beat this thing with the Lord's help. As the spring ended and turned into summer, one month of sobriety became two, and then three. As I approached the fourth month, I became nervous. It had been towards the end of the third month of sobriety, two years before, where I had taken that drink that started my relapse.

As the day approached, I prayed for more strength and reached out to my network of Christian men for support. I confided in them my fears and they prayed for me and I drew strength from their encouragement. I shared my fears with my counselor and he prayed for me too. During that entire third month, I made sure that I didn't have a single idle moment. I needed to occupy all of my time so that I would not cave in a moment of weakness and take a drink. The days turned into weeks and before I knew it, the third month had passed and I was still sober. I thanked God from the bottom of my heart for giving me the grace and courage to stay clean.

I had reached a major milestone. This was uncharted territory for me. At that point in my life, it was the longest period of time in fourteen years that I had been sober, military training and deployments notwithstanding. It was truly remarkable. I felt that *we* had accomplished something together, me and the Lord. Something big and profound had taken place in my life that could only be explained through the transforming power of the Holy Spirit.

Three months became six, and six months turned into a year. Then one year became two, and two became four and on it goes.

My sobriety continues to this day.

EPILOGUE

As I close this manuscript, it has been years since I took a drink. I think back on those former days and compare it to my life now, and the word *joy* keeps coming to mind. I had no joy in my former life. My former life was full of guilt, shame, and hopelessness. And alcohol. Always more alcohol. Every day was a repeat of previous miseries and failures. My health suffered. My relationships failed. My career hung on by a thread. I had no self-respect, no pride. My life seemed destined to continue in an endless rut towards complete ruin, with my mistakes on constant replay. I couldn't see a way out from the war that raged inside.

But all of that changed when I finally met Jesus Christ on his terms and began to surrender my life to Him daily and serve Him. He began the process of transforming me from the inside out. He gave me the daily courage and strength to put down the bottle for good. And He restored my joy. As Jesus said, "*These things I have spoken to you, that My joy may remain in you, and that your joy may be full*" (John 15:11 NKJV).

In addition to finding joy again, my recovery centered on redefining my identity. One of the most powerful conversations that I had with my counselor, Donn, was about identity—as in who am I? Why do I do the things I do? In who or what is my identity based?

For years I had forged an identity that was far away from God. I started out as the shy, awkward kid who was constantly trying to overcome my stutter, trying to join the "in" crowd, trying to be liked and act *like* everyone else. I developed into a college party hound, using alcohol to cut loose and feel like I fit in. I ended up wasting my potential until I decided to become a Marine. Thankfully, the transformation into a military officer and surviving three deployments kept me on the straight and narrow for periods of my life, but alcohol was always luring me back. I lost numerous relationships. After those failures, I was convinced that only one thing had stuck by me through thick and thin. Alcohol. I gave in to its hold on my life over and over. It defined my life and who I was, and who I was becoming. Alcohol cost me dearly. My identity was dictated by alcohol and it ruled me until I could bear it no longer.

I remember sitting on Donn's couch one spring afternoon as we discussed this. He looked me right in the eyes and asked me, "Who are you, Jordan? Are you a drunk? Are you a failed husband? Are you a Marine?" His questions cut me right through to the core and I felt myself choking up. *Who am I?* The answer was that I was all those things, and I felt defined by each of my failures. I struggled in terms of how the world viewed me and how I viewed myself. My definition of success had become so wrapped up in the Marine Corps that I had a hard time valuing anything outside of my Marine Corps career. My marriage falling apart had shaken me, and it now represented yet another failure. In addition, Donn's question about who I was pricked at all the feelings I had bottled up about myself since childhood—shame over my stutter, the social rejections I had faced over and over again, the overwhelming desire to fit in and be accepted, and so on.

Sitting on my counselor's chair with these thoughts

flickering through my mind, Donn then asked me, "Who are you *to Christ* and who are you *in Christ?*" Well, that question stopped me in my tracks. I had never considered my identity in terms of how God viewed me. The question made me reevaluate what God considers important. It turns out that Scripture has a lot to say about our identify in God's sight.

In his book, *Soul Physicians,* Robert Kelleman lists three pages of Bible verses that depict who we are to Christ. As I read his list of verses, I worked through my battle with alcohol and identify against what Scripture has to say. Eventually, I was inspired to create my own shortlist of Bible verses, some of his and some of my own finding, to cling to in my struggle.

In Christ,

I am a child of God. *John 1:12*
I am chosen. *John 15:16*
I am of great worth. *Luke 12:7*
I am complete in Him. *Colossians 2:10*
I am God's masterpiece. *Ephesians 2:10*
I am dearly loved. *Ephesians 5:1*
I am forgiven. *Ephesians 1:9*
I am free from condemnation. *Romans 8:1*
I am alive with Christ. *Ephesians 2:5*
I am holy and blameless. *Ephesians 1:4*
I am a citizen of heaven. *Philippians 3:20*
I am not alone. *Hebrews 13:5*
I am set free. *Romans 8:2*
I am a new creation. *2 Corinthians 5:17*
I am called by God. *2 Timothy 1:9*
I can resist the devil. *James 4:7*
I can have self-discipline. *2 Timothy 1:7*
I can overcome through faith. *1 John 5:4*
I have peace. *Ephesians 2:14*
I have new hope. *Ephesians 1:12*

Pondering the simple question, "Who are you to Christ and who are you in Christ?" is powerful. So powerful that it began to change me from the inside out once I came to know how God sees me. I came to understand that Christ is the true source of my identify and self-worth. Christ is the One who defines who I am—not the world, not my sin, and not my past.

The prompting to see myself the way God sees me made me believe that it was possible to redefine myself. I had looked for my value and standing to come from the world and I had chased after what society considers important for a long time. When you do this, it will eventually lead to emptiness and disappointment. Instead, Christ is the true source of identify. He is the One to bestow significance. When you know your worth and value to Christ, you can live your life with that confidence. You start chasing after the things of God and living your life with His priorities in mind. The knowledge of your significance in God's sight can actually drive behaviors to change.

I've come to understand that all the things I've experienced and done, both good and bad, are simply layers of my past. They do not define *who* I am or *what* I can be. I don't have to define myself as a drunk forever or live in the shadow of that identify. It's possible for me to be a completely different person and to be free. Through sincere repentance in Christ, my sins are no longer held against my account. I am truly sorry for things I've done, but my past sins have no power over me for tomorrow. My identity is in Christ and He is enough. He wipes the slate clean. Everything I have experienced is another layer to the person I have forged in the here and now, and the mistakes do not define me.

So, I ask you reader, "Who are you to Christ and who are you in Christ?" In who or what will you place your identity and self-worth? The Savior of the world longs to redeem your life to one of significance.

As my identity in Christ strengthened and took on real depth and maturity, the Lord began to restore things to my life that alcohol had once taken away. One of the most important things that I recovered was my sense of confidence and self-respect. Alcohol had taken away every last shred of pride in myself that I had, but as I embraced my new identity, one without alcohol, I found my self-respect returning little by little. As more time passed and I stayed sober, my self-confidence also increased. I no longer had a reason to hate myself or abuse myself with alcohol. I no longer felt like I was carrying around the weight of my sins on parade for all the world to see. There was no need to use alcohol to fit in. I fit in just fine without it. In fact, I came to realize that boozing was the thing that made me more of an outsider. Being constantly drunk was abnormal, but I just couldn't see that before. Without alcohol, I suddenly had so much more time and so many more possibilities open to me.

The benefits of sobriety were both mental and physical. My health returned to me. I found that I could exercise with a level of intensity that I had not experienced since my early twenties. Without alcohol, my body began to repair itself and my heart became stronger. I began to rediscover many things, great and small, that I used to enjoy. Simple things, like waking up and pouring myself a steaming hot cup of coffee took on extra significance; I did it not because I needed the caffeine to fight a hangover, but simply because I enjoyed the taste.

I rediscovered the pleasures of walking a fairway on a golf course and enjoying the hot sunshine on my face and seeing the greenery all around me. I took pleasure in scenic landscapes and beautiful skies without alcohol to cloud the enjoyment. One of my favorite moments of the day is just before the dawn. I love seeing the sky turn from inky black to deep blue, to a sleepy gray haze, and then to golden yellow with a fiery core. Through the years, I have witnessed many sunrises, mostly because I was up drinking through the night and into the morning. Now, when I have the occasion to witness a sunrise, I pause and thank God for all He has done for me.

God used several of the major events in my life, especially the ones I viewed as losses, to eventually help me course correct. For example, I initially thought that leaving my active duty career was the worst thing to happen to me, and I struggled with regret over the decision for years. In some ways, it felt like I lost myself. In reality, God used that loss as a driving force to clean up my life and rebuild my identity. It represented a break from the culture of the military where I learned to work hard, yes, but also to play hard in the form of getting wasted. Leaving active duty set certain things in motion in my life that pushed me to finally confront my drinking problem head-on. Ultimately, I learned that my source of strength and self-worth cannot be wrapped up in something even as honorable as the Marine Corps.

Other good things came from that event. I built a civilian career that I excel in and enjoy greatly. My expertise become more well-rounded, and I hit my professional stride while engaged in truly interesting projects. God threw in another bonus for me. In recent years, my profession has prompted me to do so much public speaking that my stutter has significantly decreased, something that likely would not have happened had I not been stretched professionally by my civilian career.

My Marine Corps career continued in the Reserves, and I was promoted with strong accolades. Recently, the opportunity presented to return to active duty, so the Lord has seen fit to bring me full circle. I realized that I love the Marine Corps and I proudly serve, but I love the Lord more and I give Him the credit for what he has done in my life. So as I reflect on the last several years, I see that it was all part of God's plan, and that God worked things for good in my life. The Bible says in the book of Romans: *"And we know that in all things*

God works for the good of those who love him, who have been called according to his purpose" (Romans 8:28). How amazing it is to be called by God Himself, and to be part of His purposes.

I said earlier that the word *joy* kept coming to mind. Let me add the word *relationship* to that. That word is powerful. I believe that relationships are closely tied to identity. My identity before Christ led me into meaningless and flawed relationships with the people around me, most of all with women. I used relationships as a coping mechanism or to try to fix the broken identity I'd built for myself, to try and become someone that people wanted to be around. It became a vicious circle—the wrong identity led to broken relationships which led to a worse identity and more coping attempts in all the wrong ways. I finally got off this crazy cycle when I restored my relationship with Jesus Christ. By fixing my vertical relationship with Him, I could then see clearly to start fixing my horizontal relationships with the people in my life.

Without alcohol to color things, I learned new ways to interact with people, healthier behavior patterns, and better ways to communicate—all of them so much more fulfilling and rewarding than my alcoholic ways used to be when I tried to compensate for my weaknesses. There just isn't any comparison. Knowing what I know now, I regret all of those years I wasted with alcohol.

I rediscovered the joy of connecting with family and friends. I had become a hermit because I needed to hide my drinking. With drinking behind me, I was able to reach out to my family. All of a sudden, I was available for family events and outings. I could focus on being a good friend to others, rather than simply indulging myself. Since I also found myself single again, I realized I could interact with godly women without baggage or ulterior motives for the first time. I didn't have to worry about a "good girl" finding out about my secret life. I didn't have to use alcohol to boost my confidence or create any false bravado. There were no secrets! I could actually seek out a healthy relationship without alcohol to mask the real me.

In His goodness, God brought a new woman into my life, beautiful inside and out, who fully supported my story and my sobriety. She fell in love with the real me, not who alcohol encouraged me to be. Our relationship became the first one in my life without alcohol in the mix. She is now my wife, we have a baby boy, and I've never been happier. When God is allowed to lead something, the outcome is perfect every time!

Spending time alone with God each day and developing a relationship with Him was the only true answer to the problems that I faced. I found that being in God's Word each day brought me closer to Him. The more that I prayed, the more I grew to rely on Him. As I drew closer to God, He drew closer to me. The most important lesson He taught me was that I need to go to Him *daily* for grace, courage, and forgiveness. The minute I let my guard down and became complacent was the minute that the enemy sprang his trap.

After a long and difficult journey, I feel like I finally know the secret to having contentment, joy, and a fulfilled life. Rather than pursuing an identity centered on prestige, wealth, success, or the fleeting comforts of this world, the secret is a relationship. Walking hand in hand with my Savior each and every day and pursuing His purposes for my life, not my own. Keeping constant fellowship with Him has given me the daily courage, strength and emotional endurance to put my past behind me once and for all and to press onward.

What is your story?

Perhaps you worry you have sinned too much. Maybe you think you have consumed too much alcohol or had too much illicit sex. Maybe you think you have done too many drugs, or watched too much porn, or hurt too many people. Maybe you assume that forgiveness and restoration is for other people, but not for you.

I tell you now that you are wrong. The Lord restored me

after what felt like a lifetime of drinking and excess. He met me in my mess and mended the pieces of my life that I thought were broken beyond repair. He removed the invisible chains weighing me down and gave me his yoke to bear instead: *"Come to me, all you who are weary and burdened, and I will give you rest. Take my yoke upon you and learn from me, for I am gentle and humble in heart, and you will find rest for your souls. For my yoke is easy and my burden is light"* (Matthew 11:28-30). Jesus certainly said it beautifully in my favorite passage of Scripture. I am no longer enslaved to an inner war and turmoil, and I have found that deep, long-lasting rest for my soul, as promised.

No matter the vice, no matter the depth of depravity, no matter how far from God you have wandered, there is no sin that Jesus cannot forgive. There is no life that Christ cannot restore. In fact, there is a passage of Scripture that speaks to this very thing in the most poetic way: *"Therefore He is able to save to the uttermost those who come to God through Him"* (Hebrew 7:25 NKJV).

The uttermost. That was me and my story. And it can be your story, too. So, trust Him. Repent. Let Him forgive you and your uttermost sin. Jesus is the restorer of souls. He longs to be invited into your life, and He offers hope for tomorrow. He wants to take your burdens upon Himself. He promises rest for your soul. And you will be able to drink from the true well, His well, that never runs dry.

"The Lord is not … willing that any should perish but that all should come to repentance."

— 2 Peter 3:9 NKJV

TRUTH & PRACTICE

My story is a written testament to the incredible transformative power of Jesus Christ. It is through Him alone that I found victory over alcohol and felt freedom for the first time in my life.

To experience that kind of transformative power in your own life, a personal relationship with Jesus Christ is needed. Though Jesus is always willing to meet people where they are and change them from the inside out, it is up to each individual to take that first step of faith.

We build a relationship with whatever it is we have in our hearts. For many years, alcohol was at the center of my life and priorities, and so, I built my entire world around it. I became powerless to change my habits and break free from alcohol's hold on my life. It was only when I replaced the alcohol with something (or Someone) better, that my life began to change from the inside out.

The Bible says that God created man in His own image. Meaning that of all of God's creations, humankind is the only thing that He fashioned after Himself. We can think, reason, feel emotions, accomplish great deeds, love or hate others, and so on. We do all of these things because God does these things. He imbued us with His own characteristics.

Sadly, when people deny the existence of God and strive to live for their own existence and for their own pleasure, they go against the natural purpose for which they were created. God didn't create us to pursue riches, fame, power, or selfish ambition. He created us to live in a close relationship with Himself. Since He is the ultimate source of life and existence, it follows that a relationship with Him would be one of the most natural things in the world. However, when we choose to remove God from the center of our being and pursue other interests, we go against God's original design. Emptiness and hollow pleasures are what remain.

It is in this void that evil takes root and grows and spills out into our behaviors. My relationship with alcohol is a perfect example. Instead of looking to God to fill up the emptiness in my earlier years, I chose to fill it with a life of excess. The more alcohol I consumed, the more vice was needed to fill the ever-growing void, but I never had enough. No amount of alcohol or vice can ever satisfy a person in the way that God can; we are simply not wired that way. God calls us into a relationship with Him. Only in relationship can He meet our emptiness head-on, transform us, and give us fullness of life.

God makes it easy to begin a personal relationship with Him. The book of Romans in the Bible provides a road map for what a person must do in order to begin this personal relationship with God. The first step is acknowledging that we are sinners. Much like a person with illness, we go to a doctor when we know that we are sick and we go to God when we realize we are failing on our own.

To be saved, we must acknowledge and accept that we are sinful beings in need of help. Romans 3:10 says, *"As it is written, there is none righteous, no, not one"* (NKJV). Everyone has done something wrong at one point or another. No one is perfect. Even something as seemingly innocent as telling a white lie is enough to condemn us; it is still wrong and it is still sin. Whether we have committed one sin or thousands of them, one sin is all it takes to separate us from God. This is declared in Romans 3:23, *"For all have sinned and fallen short of the glory of God"* (NKJV). All of us have fallen short and are separated from God as a consequence of sin.

But God didn't leave us to our fate of being separated from Him. He sent His own Son, Jesus Christ, a person who had never sinned at all, into our world to pay the penalty of our own short comings. Romans 5:8 states, *"But God demonstrates his own love for us in this: While we were still sinners, Christ died for us."* Jesus Christ chose to die for you and for me, to save us from ourselves.

Many of us have grown up hearing that Jesus died for us, but stop and think about it. The thought is truly profound. Soldiers will die for their country because they love and cherish it, and many would be willing to die to protect their family. Some might even die for a person who is really good, but who among us would willingly die for someone who is evil?

Yet this is exactly what Christ did for us. The Bible says that without Christ, we are eternally doomed because of our sinful ways, and yet God provided a way out for us. Scripture declares: *"For the wages of sin is death, but the gift of God is eternal life in Christ Jesus our Lord"* (Romans 6:23). Jesus Christ helps us move away from our doomed, sinful state into a perfect and eternal relationship with God.

The mechanics of this spiritual transaction are simple. It is a matter of believing and acknowledging: *"If you declare with your mouth, 'Jesus is Lord,' and believe in your heart that God raised him from the dead, you will be saved. For it is with your heart that you believe and are justified, and it is with your mouth that you profess your faith and are saved"* (Romans 10:9-10). It is that simple. Believing in your heart that Jesus was raised from the dead means that he can therefore save you too. And confessing in words that Jesus is the Lord of your life means that you are willing to turn over the reins of your life to Him and do things His way. That's it! That is what it takes to be saved. The secret to joy and to freedom can seem so elusive and yet is so easily accessible.

All of us have the same choice to make and the same opportunity. The Bible promises that *"...everyone who calls on the name of the Lord will be saved"* (Romans 10:13). And that verse truly means *everyone*. There are no favorites before God, no one is more worthy than another. Everyone has the same opportunity for salvation. When we accept His offer, He then provides us with the necessary power to defeat sin in our lives, and we don't have to go through life alone.

Jesus has promised to go before us. Scripture says this about salvation in Jesus: *"Therefore he is able, once and forever, to save those who come to God through him. He lives forever to intercede with God on their behalf"* (Hebrews 7:25 NKJV). This verse tells us that Jesus is our go-between. He died on the cross because He loved us. He gives us both hope for this life and the promise of heaven one day. It is a gift that is free for the taking, for anyone who wants to experience life and renewal and rest.

For those readers who have already accepted this incredible gift from God, it is important to remember that we are still sinners. Even as Christians, we can never stop being vigilant. The enemy will always be looking to trip us up and lead us away from God. As followers of Christ, we are called to live like Jesus Christ would have lived. But since all men and women have an inherent sin nature, we will make mistakes and we will stumble from time to time. When we do, God tells us to confess our sins to Him and He will be faithful to forgive us. *"If we confess our sins, he is faithful and just and will forgive us our sins and purify us from all unrighteousness"* (1 John 1:9).

Confession of sin is the first step to having a right relationship with God, and it brings us to a place of forgiveness. Step number two is repentance. Repentance is the follow-on action to being forgiven and represents a person making a one hundred and eighty degree turn from the sinful behaviors of the past and going in a completely different direction.

To illustrate the connection between forgiveness and repentance, I recall a sermon I once heard that used the term, *critical mass*, to make the case for true, biblical repentance. The term was used in the context of a chemical reaction. Once something has accelerated past a certain point, it's at critical mass. In order to repent, we first have to recognize our own sinfulness and ask forgiveness from God. We invite Jesus into our hearts to save us and lead us forward. But in order for the sinner's prayer to take hold and accomplish its purpose—in other words, propel us forward into critical mass—we must follow up our prayer with action and literally turn away from our sin.

What good would it do to pray and beg for God's mercy and forgiveness and then willfully keep on sinning? By the person's own choices, it would be evident that the person was not serious at all. We show how serious we are about our faith by how we conduct ourselves on this earth. We act according to what we have resolved to do in our hearts. Repentance is a call to action, not rote prayers and empty promises. A sinner's prayer combined with true repentance has the power to save a person's soul and change their life. The action of turning away from our sin causes our faith to reach critical mass and take hold in our lives.

In my case, true repentance meant putting the bottle down and literally turning away from that behavior and lifestyle and never going back. I couldn't dabble with alcohol and tell myself that I could control it and only have one or two drinks. Fourteen years of alcohol abuse had proved that notion wrong. I needed new boundaries. Repentance for me was staying out of bars, happy hours, and places where alcohol was available. It meant not keeping beer and wine in the house for when the occasional guest came over and avoiding gatherings where alcohol would be abundant. It meant a total and clean break from alcohol and the lifestyle that goes with it. Instead of drinking, I replaced alcohol with God. I began a vibrant prayer life. I studied the Bible. I memorized Bible verses so that I could defend myself against enemy attacks. In short, I filled myself up with Jesus Christ and the Holy Spirit.

As I did this, I became a different person. The process is described beautifully in God's Word: *"Therefore if anyone is in Christ, he is a new creation; old things have passed away; behold, all things have become new"* (2 Corinthians 5:17 NKJV). When a person accepts Jesus Christ, their past has been forgiven and they have a new purpose in life. Simply put, Jesus Christ moves into a person's life and begins to change them from the inside out. The Bible also calls us to take an active role in the transformation process: *"Do not conform to the pattern of this world, but be transformed by the renewing of your mind. Then you will be able to test and approve what God's will is—his good, pleasing and perfect will"* (Romans 12:2). We are called to live differently. We are not to conform to the ways of the world. When we are in lock step with God and His ways, the Holy Spirit can change the way we think and give us the power to change behavior.

In my case, I was able to admit that my drinking was destroying my life and that it was a symptom of a deeper problem. When I finally came to God, He filled the void and I steadily gained the strength and motivation to change my behavior once and for all. However, even though I was changing my outward actions, it was a slower process to change the way I actually thought and felt about alcohol inside. During my first sober period, the one that was ultimately unsuccessful, I missed alcohol and thought about it all the time. I was staying sober, but I was constantly fighting for it mentally and it was exhausting. I just couldn't seem to get alcohol out of my head, and regrettably I had my relapse three months later.

At that time, I thought to myself, *what happened? What went wrong? Did I not do something correctly? Why am I still struggling with this?* I wanted to have a dramatic transformation and lead a dramatically transformed life, but it seemed to be eluding me. For years I had no answer. Then I began to see a counselor at my church, and I poured my heart out to him. I voiced fears about relapsing and not being able to get sober again, and I asked him where I was going wrong in the transformation process. During one of our sessions, my counselor said something to me that I will never forget. He said, "Jordan, maybe not everyone is going to have a dramatic transformation experience. Not everyone is called to a high-profile ministry through a dramatic series of events. What if God wants to transform the average person by having them repent and come to Him for transformation every single day?"

I don't think my counselor realized it, but his statement hit me like a freight train and I was sure he had just said in one sentence what I had been trying to figure out for years. I had been looking at characters in the Bible and Christian leaders around me with the misconception that they were somehow made of different material than I was. Like they had some extra DNA that allowed them to lead powerful Christian lives, while I was down in the trenches getting crushed. During my relapse, I saw examples of godly men living their lives with enormous power and conviction, yet I couldn't seem to put the bottle down. I was so discouraged and thought maybe I hadn't trusted God enough, or repented enough, and that I would never be good enough.

The answer was that I had been looking to God for a dramatic transformation, as if a lightning bolt would come down from heaven and transform me all at once. Instead, I needed to learn that real transformation and repentance is accomplished each and every day. I had to learn the rhythm of coming to God in humility each day and asking for forgiveness and healing. Daily and sometimes even hourly, I prayed for His sustaining grace to help me turn away from my sin that day.

It took me committing to a daily walk with Christ to finally overcome my daily struggle with alcohol. God wasn't offering me a quick-fix solution; he was offering me a completely new way of life. I hope that this truth can give hope to average people struggling with their sin. When we come to God each day, He will sustain us and give us the grace and strength to live the Christian life. I simply needed to get out of the way and let the Holy Spirit do His transformative work.

The Bible says that when we accept Jesus Christ as our Savior, God sends His Holy Spirit to live inside of us and guide us. This process begins the transforming work of the Holy Spirit in our lives. We just have to be receptive to the Holy Spirit's leading. The Holy Spirit stands ready to help us through difficulties and temptations that we encounter. The Bible calls us to "...*walk in the Spirit, then you will not fulfill the lusts of the flesh*" (Galatians 5:16 NKJV). I remember coming across that verse and thinking how it cut right to my problem. If I could learn to walk in the Spirit, then perhaps I could withstand the urge to drink.

But how does one walk in the Spirit? It certainly took me a while to figure it out and embrace the answer. I learned to walk in the Spirit by spending time in the Bible and coming to a new understanding of who God is. It meant submitting to His lordship over my life and seeking His direction for every decision I faced. Gradually, I came to rely on the Lord and seek His ways first. I started living my life according to what the Bible says, and not trying to go it alone using my own human reasoning and effort.

At the heart of it, walking in the Spirit is about developing a relationship with Him, not just dropping by once a month for a quick conversation. A husband and wife spend time with each other, converse often, and get to know all about the other person. In the same way, I found that the more time I spent in the Bible and the more time I devoted to prayer, the more I *knew* God and could sense His presence and guidance in my life. Then when temptations to drink came along, it was easier to knock them back down. I had Jesus with me to do the fighting for me. I can only imagine what may have happened if I had to fight that battle on my own. Instead, His power was sufficient for me.

God's power manifests itself in many different ways. The examples of God's power are displayed throughout the Bible and are too numerous to discuss here, but one of my favorite examples is found in Hebrews 4:12. This verse talks about the power of God's written Word and was one of the first verses I memorized to fight the urge to drink: *"For the Word of God is living and powerful, and sharper than any two-edged sword, piercing even to the division of soul and spirit, and of joints and marrow, and is a discerner of the thoughts and intents of the heart"* (Hebrews 4:12 NKJV). This verse speaks straight to the condition of the human heart and how the Word of God illuminates and discerns our behavior.

God's Word certainly shed light on my excuses for drinking. I had come up with all kinds of excuses over the years to justify drinking. I told myself that I needed it to fit in. That I deserved it because I needed to be true to myself. That I worked hard in the Marines and drinking was a weekend reward. Or that I needed to drink to come out of my shell and be social. All of these things were excuses that I told myself so that I would not have to face the truth about my problem. When I was finally broken and I began to read the Bible, all of these lies were shattered. True to the verse, the Word of God illuminated the lies and showed me a way out.

The book of Ephesians in the Bible paints a beautiful illustration of the spiritual truths that help us wage war against the lies of the enemy. The passage calls us to put on the "full armor of God" in order to fight the personal and

inner battles we face. The deep meaning behind each piece of
armor holds promise for every believer:

> *"Finally, be strong in the Lord and in his mighty power. Put on
> the full armor of God, so that you can take your stand against
> the devil's schemes. For our struggle is not against flesh and
> blood, but against the rulers, against the authorities, against the
> powers of this dark world and against the spiritual forces of evil
> in the heavenly realms. Therefore put on the full armor of God,
> so that when the day of evil comes, you may be able to stand your
> ground, and after you have done everything, to stand. Stand firm
> then, with the belt of truth buckled around your waist, with the
> breastplate of righteousness in place, and with your feet fitted
> with the readiness that comes from the gospel of peace. In
> addition to all this, take up the shield of faith, with which you
> can extinguish all the flaming arrows of the evil one. Take the
> helmet of salvation and the sword of the Spirit, which is the
> word of God."*

— EPHESIANS 6:10-17

I thought this passage was fantastic. I could certainly
appreciate all the military references. Each piece of armor
speaks to a different truth about God's power and the
protection He offers. The "belt of truth" represents the
absolutes we know to be true—God's promises to us. At the
time of the writing of the passage, the belt would hold a
Roman soldier's gear together; in the same way, God's
promises hold us together. The "breastplate of righteousness"
symbolizes a life full of holy obedience to God's commands.
The "shoes of the gospel of peace" mean that we are ready to
live out our faith, ready to face each day, because we have the
assurance and peace that comes from knowing that our
salvation is in Christ. The "shield of faith" can be raised to
deflect and absorb the enemy attacks, symbolizing that our

faith gives us the emotional endurance to get through another day without falling to temptation. The "helmet of salvation" protects our minds because we know that our home is not here on earth, but in Heaven, and because we know the truth, we are not easily swayed by worldly promises that fall short.

Each piece of armor represents a piece of the Christian life and is designed to protect a different part of our spiritual bodies. But notice how each piece of armor is defensive in nature. These pieces protect us from the enemy and from sin. The only offensive weapon listed in the passage is the "sword of the Spirit," which is the Word of God, the Bible. This tool is our defense against temptation and being led astray by the enemy. This is why memorizing Bible verses and using them in moments of weakness is so effective. In fact, it is a technique employed by Jesus Christ Himself.

Before Jesus began his earthly ministry, he spent 40 days and nights fasting in the desert. His human nature was pushed to the limits of physical endurance. He was starving and dehydrated. When he was at his weakest point, the Devil came to tempt him to sin. With each new temptation placed before him, Jesus quoted Scripture right back to the devil and overcame the temptation. If quoting Scripture during temptation worked for Jesus, why wouldn't it help you or me too? When I relied on my 3x5 notecards and called up Bible verses to help me, I was combating the temptation and desire to drink with the Word of God, and it worked every time.

The Word of God is our most powerful weapon. In fact, Jesus Christ is the manifestation of the Word of God, according to the Gospel of John: *"In the beginning was the Word, and the Word was with God, and the Word was God"* (John 1:1). The verse is referring to Jesus Christ as God's Word, saying that He existed in the beginning and created everything. The verse says that Jesus Christ is God Himself and He is the physical representation of the spoken Word of God. So, when we apply this knowledge of Jesus to the concept of fighting temptation using the Word of God, what better weapon could we have than literally quoting Jesus into the face of temptation? No evil in the universe can defeat that!

During my journey to sobriety, as I read through the Bible, certain verses seemed to leap off the page at me. I think it is no coincidence that these verses directly addressed alcohol, living in the Spirit, walking by faith, and how to become a new creature in Christ. I wrote the verses down on 3x5 note cards and quoted them aloud repeatedly to instill them in my heart and mind. Whenever a powerful urge to drink came along, I was ready to fight back with a memorized verse or a pocketful of Scripture.

My "pocketful of Scripture" is included for you below, and I encourage you to write them out on your own notecards. I consulted various translations of the ancient text for these verses and chose to cite my favorite translations below, verse by verse. I encourage you to reference the various translations also for a richer experience with the Scripture. The Bible Gateway website (http://www.thebiblegateway.com) and the Bible Gateway App for your electronic devices is a great place to start!

I pray these verses will be a help to you on your journey.

> **Genesis 1:26** Then God said, "Let Us make man in Our image, according to Our likeness…" (NKJV).

> **Psalm 34:17-19** The righteous cry out, and the Lord hears them; he delivers them from all their troubles. The Lord is close to the brokenhearted and saves those who are crushed in spirit. The righteous person may have many troubles, but the Lord delivers him from them all (NIV).

Psalm 119:105 Your word is a lamp to my feet and a light to my path (NKJV).

Proverbs 3:5-6 Trust in the Lord with all your heart, And lean not on your own understanding; In all your ways acknowledge Him, And He shall direct your paths (NKJV).

Proverbs 20:1 Wine is a mocker, strong drink is a brawler, and whoever is led astray by it is not wise (NKJV).

Proverbs 23:29-33 Who has woe? Who has sorrow? Who has contentions? Who has complaints? Who has wounds without cause? Who has redness of eyes? Those who linger long at the wine, those who go in search of mixed wine. Do not look on the wine when it is red, when it sparkles in the cup, when it swirls around smoothly. At the last it bites like a serpent, and stinks like a viper. Your eyes will see strange things, and your heart will utter perverse things (NKJV).

Isaiah 5:11 Woe to those who rise early in the morning to run after their drinks, who stay up late at night till they are inflamed with wine (NIV).

Isaiah 5:22 Woe to those who are heroes at drinking wine and champions at mixing drinks (NIV).

Isaiah 28:7 And these also stagger from wine and reel from beer: Priests and prophets stagger from beer and are befuddled with wine; they reel from beer, they stagger when seeing visions, they stumble when rendering decisions (NIV).

Jeremiah 29:11 For I know the plans I have for you," declares the Lord, "plans to prosper you and not to harm you, plans to give you hope and a future (NIV).

Matthew 4:4 But He answered and said, "It is written, 'Man shall not live by bread alone, but by every word that proceeds from the mouth of God'" (NKJV).

Matthew 11:28-30 Come to me, all you who are weary and burdened, and I will give you rest. Take my yoke upon you and learn from me, for I am gentle and humble in heart, and you will find rest for your souls. For my yoke is easy and my burden is light (NIV).

Luke 1:37 For with God nothing will be impossible (NKJV).

Luke 5:31-32 Jesus answered them, "It is not the healthy who need a doctor, but the sick. I have not come to call the righteous, but sinners to repentance" (NIV).

Luke 21:34 But watch yourselves lest your hearts be weighed down with dissipation and drunkenness and cares of this life, and that day come upon you suddenly like a trap (ESV).

Acts 2:38 Then Peter said to them, "Repent, and let every one of you be baptized in the name of Jesus Christ for the remission of sins; and you shall receive the gift of the Holy Spirit (NKJV).

Romans 5:1 Therefore, since we have been made right in God's sight by faith, we have peace with God because of what Jesus Christ our Lord has done for us (NLT).

Romans 8:1 There is therefore now no condemnation to those who are in Christ Jesus, who do not walk according to the flesh, but according to the Spirit (NKJV).

Romans 8:7-8 The mind governed by the flesh is hostile to God; it does not submit to God's law, nor can it do so. Those who are in the realm of the flesh cannot please God (NIV).

Romans 9:16 So then it depends not on human will or exertion, but on God, who has mercy (ESV).

Romans 10:17 So then faith comes by hearing, and hearing by the word of God (NKJV).

Romans 12:1-2 Therefore, I urge you, brothers and sisters, in view of God's mercy, to offer your bodies as a living sacrifice, holy and pleasing to God—this is your true and proper worship. Do not conform to the pattern of this world, but be transformed by the renewing of your mind. Then you will be able to test and approve what God's will is—his good, pleasing and perfect will (NIV).

Romans 13:13-14 Let us behave decently, as in the daytime, not in carousing and drunkenness, not in sexual immorality and debauchery, not in dissension and jealousy. Rather, clothe yourselves with the Lord Jesus Christ, and do not think about how to gratify the desires of the flesh (NIV).

Romans 15:13 May the God of hope fill you with all joy and peace in believing, so that by the power of the Holy Spirit you may abound in hope (ESV).

1 Corinthians 2:5 So that your faith might not rest in the wisdom of men but in the power of God (ESV).

1 Corinthians 2:14 The person without the Spirit does not accept the things that come from the Spirit of God but considers them foolishness, and cannot understand them because they are discerned only through the Spirit (NIV).

1 Corinthians 6:10 Nor thieves nor the greedy nor drunkards nor slanderers nor swindlers will inherit the kingdom of God (NIV).

1 Corinthians 6:19-20 Do you not know that your bodies are temples of the Holy Spirit, who is in you, whom you have received from God? You are not your own; you were bought at a price. Therefore honor God with your bodies (NIV).

1 Corinthians 10:13 No temptation has overtaken you except what is common to mankind. And God is faithful; he will not let you be tempted beyond what you can bear. But when you are tempted, he will also provide a way out so that you can endure it (NIV).

2 Corinthians 4:16 Therefore we do not lose heart. Though outwardly we are wasting away, yet inwardly we are being renewed day by day (NIV).

2 Corinthians 5:7 For we walk by faith, not by sight (NKJV).

2 Corinthians 5:17 Therefore, if anyone is in Christ, he is a new creation; old things have passed away; behold, all things have become new (NKJV).

2 Corinthians 10:5 We destroy arguments and every lofty opinion raised against the knowledge of God, and take every thought captive to obey Christ (ESV).

Galatians 2:20 I have been crucified with Christ. It is no longer I who live, but Christ who lives in me. And the life I now live in the flesh I live by faith in the Son of God, who loved me and gave himself for me (ESV).

Galatians 5:1 It is for freedom that Christ has set us free. Stand firm, then, and do not let yourselves be burdened again by a yoke of slavery (NIV).

Galatians 5:13 You, my brothers and sisters, were called to be free. But do not use your freedom to indulge the flesh; rather, serve one another humbly in love (NIV).

Galatians 5:16-17 But I say, walk by the Spirit, and you will not gratify the desires of the flesh. For the desires of the flesh are against the Spirit, and the desires of the Spirit are against the flesh, for these are opposed to each other, to keep you from doing the things you want to do (ESV).

Galatians 5:22-23 But the fruit of the Spirit is love, joy, peace, patience, kindness, goodness, faithfulness, gentleness, self-control; against such things there is no law (ESV).

Ephesians 2:8 For by grace you have been saved through faith. And this is not your own doing; it is the gift of God, not a result of works, so that no one may boast. For we are his workmanship, created in Christ Jesus for good works, which God prepared beforehand, that we should walk in them. (ESV).

Ephesians 4:21-24 Since you have heard about Jesus and have learned the truth that comes from him, throw off your old sinful nature and your former way of life, which is corrupted by lust and deception. Instead, let the Spirit renew your thoughts and attitudes. Put on your new nature, created to be like God—truly righteous and holy (NLT).

Ephesians 5:18 Don't be drunk with wine, because that will ruin your life. Instead, be filled with the Holy Spirit (NLT).

Ephesians 6:10-11 Finally, be strong in the Lord and in his mighty power. Put on the full armor of God, so that you can take your stand against the devil's schemes (NIV).

Ephesians 6:16 In all circumstances take up the shield of faith, with which you can extinguish all the flaming darts of the evil one (ESV).

Ephesians 6:18 And pray in the Spirit on all occasions with all kinds of prayers and requests. With this in mind, be alert and always keep on praying for all the Lord's people (NIV).

Philippians 3:9 And be found in him, not having a righteousness of my own that comes from the law, but that which is through faith in Christ—the righteousness that comes from God on the basis of faith (NIV).

Philippians 4:6-7 Be anxious for nothing, but in everything by prayer and supplication, with thanksgiving, let your requests be made known to God; and the peace of God, which surpasses all understanding, will guard your hearts and minds through Christ Jesus (NKJV).

Philippians 4:13 I can do all things through Christ who strengthens me (NKJV).

1 Timothy 1:19 Cling to your faith in Christ, and keep your conscience clear. For some people have deliberately violated their consciences; as a result, their faith has been shipwrecked (NLT).

1 Timothy 6:12 Fight the good fight of the faith. Take hold of the eternal life to which you were called when you made your good confession in the presence of many witnesses (NIV).

2 Timothy 1:7 For God gave us a spirit, not of fear, but of power and love and self-control (ESV).

2 Timothy 2:22 Flee the evil desires of youth and pursue righteousness, faith, love and peace, along with those who call on the Lord out of a pure heart (NIV).

Titus 2:12-14 And we are instructed to turn from godless living and sinful pleasures. We should live in this evil world with wisdom, righteousness, and devotion to God, while we look forward with hope to that wonderful day when the glory of our great God and Savior, Jesus Christ, will be revealed. He gave his life to free us from every kind of sin, to cleanse us, and to make us his very own people, totally committed to doing good deeds (NLT).

Hebrews 4:12 For the word of God is living and powerful, sharper than any two-edged sword, piercing to the division of soul and of spirit, of joints and of marrow, and discerning the thoughts and intentions of the heart (NKJV).

Hebrews 7:25 Therefore He is able to save to the uttermost those who come to God through Him (NKJV).

Hebrews 11:1 Now faith is the assurance of things hoped for, the conviction of things not seen (ESV).

James 1:5-6 If you need wisdom, ask our generous God, and he will give it to you. He will not rebuke you for asking. But when you ask him, be sure that your faith is in God alone. Do not waver, for a person with divided loyalty is as unsettled as a wave of the sea that is blown and tossed by the wind (NLT).

James 1:12-15 God blesses those who patiently endure testing and temptation. Afterward they will receive the crown of life that God has promised to those who love him. And remember, when you are being tempted, do not say, "God is tempting me." God is never tempted to do wrong and he never tempts anyone else. Temptation comes from our own desires, which entice us and drag us away. These desires give birth to sinful actions. And when sin is allowed to grow, it gives birth to death (NIV).

James 1:21 So get rid of all the filth and evil in your lives, and humbly accept the word God has planted in your hearts, for it has the power to save your souls (NLT).

James 4:6 And he gives grace generously. As the Scriptures say, "God opposes the proud but gives grace to the humble" (NLT).

James 4:7 Submit yourselves therefore to God. Resist the devil, and he will flee from you (ESV).

James 5:16 Confess your trespasses to one another, and pray for one another, that you may be healed. The effective, fervent prayer of a righteous man avails much (NKJV).

1 Peter 2:24 He himself bore our sins in his body on the tree, that we might die to sin and live to righteousness. By his wounds you have been healed (ESV).

1 Peter 5:8 Be sober, be vigilant; because your adversary the devil walks about like a roaring lion, seeking whom he may devour (NKJV).

2 Peter 3:9 The Lord is not slack concerning His promise, as some count slackness, but is longsuffering toward us, not willing that any should perish but that all should come to repentance (NKJV).

1 John 1:9 If we confess our sins, he is faithful and just to forgive us our sins and to cleanse us from all unrighteousness (NKJV).

1 John 5:4 For everyone who has been born of God overcomes the world. And this is the victory that has overcome the world—our faith (ESV).

Revelation 3:20 Behold, I stand at the door and knock. If anyone hears my voice and opens the door, I will come in… (ESV).

75671184R00159

Made in the USA
Columbia, SC
19 September 2019